Praise for Annie Wilder's
House of Spirits and Whispers

Gripping and reassuringly believable … *House of Spirits
and Whispers* is a well-paced, engaging love story of a
woman and a house—each spirited in its own way.
Ghost! Magazine

Whether or not you believe in ghosts, you'll enjoy *House of Spirits
and Whispers*. It's a pleasure to spend time with a good storyteller—
one gifted with style, wit, and compassionate insight.
MindSpring.com

For a fine reading experience, and another look at the
paranormal and its secrets, Annie Wilder gives you a top-notch,
first-rate journey into the unknown … splendid reading.
GhostVillage.com

Who doesn't wish to discover the secrets of their home?
Right from the beginning readers will be
hooked. A fascinating tale, well told.
BookReview.com

spirits
out of time

Annie Wilder is a writer and the mother of grown children. She hosts haunted tea parties at her ghost-filled Victorian house in a historic Mississippi River town in Minnesota. *House of Spirits and Whispers,* her first book, is a true account of her experiences living with ghosts. Visit her online at www.anniewilder.com.

annie wilder

spirits
out of time

*true family ghost stories
and weird paranormal
experiences*

LLEWELLYN PUBLICATIONS
woodbury, minnesota

FIRST EDITION
First Printing, 2009

Book design by Rebecca Zins
Cover design by Kevin R. Brown
Cover frame: istockphoto; cuckoo clock: PhotoDisc
Cover photo of Maggie, Dorrie, and Mimi McDonough,
and all interior photos unless otherwise specified, are courtesy of the author
Photo on page 168 by Lynne Menturweck

Llewellyn is a registered trademark of Llewellyn Worldwide, Ltd.

Library of Congress Cataloging-in-Publication Data
Wilder, Annie, 1961-
    Spirits out of time : true family ghost stories and weird paranormal experiences /
Annie Wilder.
       p. cm.
    Includes bibliographical references (p.   ) and index.
    ISBN 978-0-7387-1440-0
    1. Ghosts. I. Title.
    BF1461.W53 2009
    133.1—dc22

                                                          2009019120

Llewellyn Worldwide does not participate in, endorse, or have any authority or responsibility concerning private business transactions between our authors and the public.

    All mail addressed to the author is forwarded but the publisher cannot, unless specifically instructed by the author, give out an address or phone number.

    Any Internet references contained in this work are current at publication time, but the publisher cannot guarantee that a specific location will continue to be maintained. Please refer to the publisher's website for links to authors' websites and other sources.

Llewellyn Publications
A Division of Llewellyn Worldwide, Ltd.
2143 Wooddale Drive, Dept. 978-0-7387-1440-0
Woodbury, MN 55125-2989
www.llewellyn.com

Printed in the United States of America

CONTENTS

This book is dedicated to my dad's brother Larry
and my mom's sister Margie.
It is also dedicated to my cousin Stephanie (Alexandra).

ACKNOWLEDGMENTS

Iwish to thank everyone who contributed a story or photograph or their time to this book. Great-Aunt Clara shared wonderful stories of her grandma Wieland (my great-great-grandma) and was a joy to talk to—thanks, Clara, for all the help and the pictures and poem. Great-Aunt Irene graciously gave permission to include her ghost stories and some of her experiences living in the Irish family homestead. My aunt Margie, along with my mom's cousins Bev and Kay, and my daughter Molly, helped Irene and me with proofing and filling in details.

My mom, Aunt Margie, and Aunt Kathy were a tremendous help with pictures and stories from the Irish side of the family, and my dad provided detailed and entertaining answers to dozens of email queries about the Montana side of the family. Thanks to my siblings and their spouses/significant others, my nieces and nephews, and my kids Molly and Jack for sharing your stories.

I want to extend special thanks to my friend and fellow writer Jennifer Spees for reading my manuscript and for her excellent suggestions, and to my daughter Molly for helping organize and manage the permissions process. To my beau and partner Levi, thanks for the emotional support, the many hours of proofing and reading, and for all the cooking!

Several psychics and other paranormal or metaphysical professionals granted permission to use their names and stories in my book—thank you Robert Baca, Echo Bodine, Lori Bogren, Linda Drake, James Endredy, Ted Hughes, Jodi Livon, Patrick Mathews, Dave Schrader,

C. J. Sellars, Mary Stoffel, and Mary Ann Winkowski. Thank you to Ivy for letting me use the India ghost photo, and Linda and Jim at the Historic Trempealeau Hotel and Roger at Magus Books for letting me include the names of your business establishments in my story. Cindy Thury Smith at the City of Hastings Pioneer Room spent many hours helping me do research for the ghost book that wasn't ready to be written—yet. Thank you, Cindy, for all the help and for providing the picture of Katrina Hartnett that appears in this book.

I truly appreciate my mom's cousin Margie's permission to tell her daughter Stephanie's story in the chapter on animal spirits and messengers.

Thanks to my friend Vanessa Wright and everyone at Llewellyn who helped make my book a reality, especially Jeanette Jones for doing a great job with all of the interior photographs, Lynne Menturweck for taking the photograph for the White Deer chapter opener, and Kevin Brown for the extra help with the cover photo of Maggie, Dorrie, and Mimi McDonough. A huge thanks goes out to my editor and friend Becky Zins for lending her talent and creativity to this project.

Finally, I'd like to express my deep appreciation to my uncle Larry and aunt Margie, who each gave our family a wonderful and lasting gift: they collected our family stories and wrote them down.

. . . . . .

This book is a true recollection and account of ghostly or paranormal phenomena that my family and I have experienced, and it represents, to the best of my ability, accurate retellings of real events. Some of the names in the book have been changed for privacy.

Stories can conquer fear, you know.
They can make the heart bigger.
Ben Okri

❧

Introduction

I have always been fascinated by secrets. And I've always been drawn to stories with elements of magic and death and drama. Maybe it's my Irish blood, my twelfth-house moon, or the intuitive awareness, even as a child, that there was much, much more going on around us than was acknowledged at school or on TV. As a child, I loved grippingly sad fairy tales—*Babes in the Wood*, *The Little Mermaid*, and *The Little Match Girl* were among my favorites, along with the decidedly less grim picture-book adventures of Dorrie, the Little Witch. I love ghost stories, especially true ones, which is part of the reason I have been perfectly happy living in a haunted house for the last fifteen years. I wrote about my experiences living with ghosts in my first book, *House of Spirits and Whispers*.

This book is a collection of family ghost stories and lore. Some of these stories I only learned about after my first book came out. Other stories I've heard—or heard snippets of—since I was a child. I figured out early that the best time to hear the most interesting stories was by hanging around the grownups when there weren't any other kids around—at fancy family parties when the after-dinner cordials were served, or in the kitchen while the grownups took turns at washing dishes. Many of the stories come from my mom's Irish relatives. My Irish grandma, whom

I adored, told us about fairies, or "little people," and banshees and Irish beliefs regarding death, like the death knock that would be heard just before someone in the house died. My Irish great-grandmother told my mom stories about the fairies that had come over from Ireland, hidden in the trunks of the people coming to start a new life in America. And my mom, who can see and hear spirits, was followed around for decades by the ghost of a young girl. It was only recently that she learned the spirit girl's surprising identity.

On my dad's side of the family, his German relatives had some memorable precognitive experiences. These experiences almost always involved either love or death, like my great-great-grandma Wieland seeing a falling star each time one of her children died. (She lost six of her thirteen children.) Her daughter, my great-grandma Schultz, had a vivid dream of a tragic event—which she discovered the next day had come true. And my dad's father, a Montana farmer, just "knew things," like one time being aware that there had been a car accident on the road behind him and that he needed to go back and help the people involved. My Montana grandpa also came back to visit my grandma after he died.

My parents' house has a few ghosts of its own. My mom and dad have lived there for thirty-some years, and it seems to be getting more and more haunted as time goes by. There's a smoking ghost, the spirit of my mom's dog George, and even a ghost who strummed a guitar in my parents' bedroom one night.

Along with our family ghost stories are true accounts of odd or mystical experiences that I've had throughout my life, as well as some of the weirdest and most interesting stories I've heard at book events I've attended and haunted tea parties I've hosted. More often than not, people preface their story by saying, "I've never told anyone this before, but ..."

I've learned that it's not that people don't have ghost stories, it's that they usually don't tell them. Their encounters with the spirit world are hidden away, doubted, denied. But like ghosts themselves, they're never quite completely gone.

All of the stories in this book are true, all fall outside the realm of commonplace reality, and hopefully, all of them reveal at least some of the secrets of the spirit realm, that invisible world of untold stories.

Irish Branch

Great-Great-Grandparents: Patrick McDonough and his first wife, Bridget, had nine children in Ireland. When Bridget died, Patrick got married again. Patrick and his second wife, Mary, immigrated to America. Their children: my great-grandma Maggie, Kate, Annie, and a baby who died.

Great-Grandparents: Maggie McDonough married Thomas Gherty. Their children: Mimi, my grandma Dorrie, James, Thomas, Norah, Ethel, Ethel's twin, John, who died as a baby, Nellie, and another baby named John who died.

    Mimi remained single.

    Thomas married Irene.

    Norah married Victor Lichtenstein.

        Their children: Victor II, Penny, Bev, Kay. Kay is the mother of Kylie.

        Nellie married Harry Schaefer.

        Their child: Margie. Margie is the mother of three children, including my cousin Stephanie.

Grandparents: Dorrie married Anton Haraldson.

    Their children: Dorothy (my mom), Veronica, Anton II, Margie, Kathy, and Jerry.

        Anton II is the father of Clint.

        Kathy is the mother of Sigrid, Eli, and Stuart.

        Jerry is married to Diana.

Montana Branch

Great-Great-Grandparents: B. T. McClaine married Tiny Gramma (Mary Ann). B. T.'s parents were second-generation emigrants from Ireland, and Mary Ann's parents had emigrated from Scotland. B. T. and Tiny Gramma had four children, including my great-grandma Cora.

Great-Great-Grandparents: David Morgan from England and his wife, Amelia, immigrated to Canada. They had ten children, including my great-grandpa David Morgan II.

Great-Grandparents: Cora McClain married David Morgan II. They had five children, including my grandpa Bernard Morgan.

Southern Minnesota Branch

Great-Great-Grandparents: Elizabeth Wieland and her husband, Henry, had thirteen children, including my great-grandma Edith and her brother, Uncle Henry.

Great-Great-Grandparents: George Schultz and his wife, Mary, had five children, including my great-grandpa William.

Great-Grandparents: William Schultz married Edith Wieland.
    Their children: my grandma Mae, Floyd, and Clara.

Grandparents: Bernard Morgan married Mae Schultz.
    Their children: Don (my dad), Larry, Sister, and Jim.

Parents: My mom and dad are Dorothy and Don.
    Their children: Iris, Thomas, me, Betsy, Randall, Maggie, Dan, and Sam.
        Iris is the mother of Sophia and Gwendolyn.
        I am the mother of Molly and Jack.
        Betsy and **Mitch** are the parents of Christine.
        Maggie and **Rob** are the parents of the twins Oscar and Carter.
        Sam and **Jenny** are the parents of Mahala and Ava.

Halloween, 1963, Ottawa, Minnesota. Left to right:
me, my brother Thomas, and my sister Iris.

Courage is fear that has said its prayers.
Dorothy Bernard

ᏬᎥᏬ

The Yellow Eyes and
Other Experiences
from Childhood

In most ways, my childhood in the 1960s was not only happy but typical. I lived with my mom and dad and six brothers and sisters in southern Minnesota, in an old farmhouse off County Road 23. We had a big yard with a tire swing and a sandbox, several cats and a few dogs, and a blue-eyed albino horse named Trigger who lived to be thirty-three years old. (We attributed Trigger's longevity to his easygoing nature and slow metabolism.) There was a wooded area behind our house and a field beside it in which our neighbors grew corn some years and soybeans in others. I was fascinated enough by the cornfield to get lost in it once or twice, eventually making my way to our neighbors, the Schweigerts, who gave me orange juice and called my parents. We had a horseshoe-shaped driveway that was great for learning to ride a two-wheeler bike or pulling around a wagon full of dolls. A railroad track ran along the other side of County Road 23, close enough to our house that if we stood at the end of our driveway and waved, the engineer would wave back.

But even some of our childhood pastimes reflected a love of the magical or macabre. One of our favorite games was Bloody Town, a game we made up in which we pretended to be a nice family who got attacked by bloody skeletons. We played Bloody Town in our family station wagon, and although the basic premise never changed—it inevitably ended in a rollicking screamfest—we never got tired of it. Another game we played was a ghostly hybrid of tag and hide-and-seek. The people who were not "it" had to make their way around the dark yard chanting, "One o'clock, the ghost is not out; two o'clock, the ghost is not out" and so on, until the ghost came shrieking out of his or her hiding spot, trying to tag someone and turn them into a ghost, too. Eventually, there was only one unlucky person left who wasn't a ghost, and that person had to walk around the house alone while an entire horde of ghosts hid in wait.

We also had a scary story ritual: the liver story. My mom only told the story after all of us kids had cleaned our plates on nights that we had the unanimously unpopular supper of liver and onions. In the story, a woman asked her son to go to town and pick up some liver for dinner. On the way home from the store, the boy crossed a bridge and stopped to look down at the water. As he did, the liver fell out of the bag and into the river. To avoid the consequences of his actions, the boy decided to steal the liver from a corpse in the graveyard and bring that home instead. But the corpse was not happy about its liver being stolen and cooked for someone's dinner. It came out of its grave and followed the boy home, calling, "Whooo stole my liver? Whooo stole my liver?" This spooky story had a wonderfully frightful ending. When the corpse finally caught up with the boy, my mom would grab one of us kids and yell in a corpse-y voice, "Was it YOU?"

. . . . . .

I was raised Catholic, and our religious beliefs included a spirit world that was complex and dynamic, with its own hierarchies, laws, and courtesies. Catholicism provided a framework for understanding the various relationships between the living and the dead, and it taught me that we have powerful allies in the spirit world—a lesson that has served me well living with ghosts. In our down-to-earth Midwestern family, our Catholic faith was expressed as sort of a blue-collar mysticism. The unseen world of spirits and angels and saints was real and part of every-day life, along with chores and school and TV shows. It was evident in the décor of our home, comfortably coexisting alongside homemade art and family pictures. We had guardian angel pictures in our bedrooms, holy water dispensers by the doors, and palm fronds from Palm Sunday above the doorways. A print of Salvador Dali's version of the Last Supper hung on our dining room wall. There was a statue of the Virgin Mary on the room divider and a painting of the Sacred Heart of Jesus in my parents' room. I had a beautiful rosary made of pink glass beads, which I thought was way cooler than the glow-in-the-dark plastic rosary that belonged to one of my brothers. I also had small pictures of my patron saints, St. Teresa of Ávila and the "Little Flower," St. Therese of Lisieux, whose feast days are in my birthday month of October. I knew that souls could get stuck in purgatory and that people on earth—even kids!—could help the lost souls get into heaven with their prayers. From my perspective, this kind of power was akin to magic. Along with praying for the souls in purgatory, I prayed for the starving children in the *Maryknoll* magazine; I prayed for the people in communist countries; I prayed for our milkman, who had lost his arm in a car accident. (The milkman's plight was invoked by my parents throughout our childhood if we stuck our arms out the window or otherwise misbehaved on car rides.) The most dramatic and solemn Catholic artifact in our home was a big crucifix with a hidden compartment. Inside the secret compartment were a candle and a vial of oil that were to be used to administer the last rites to a dying person. Regular people had to have these special crucifixes in their home in case someone was in danger of dying before a priest could get there.

My mom told us about the Catholic concept of limbo, too, but said she didn't believe God would keep any baby out of heaven, and that neither her mother nor her grandmother had believed in limbo, either. My mom was really good at teaching us to be open to possibilities and creating an atmosphere in our home that fostered creativity, imagination, and artistic expression. We spent as much time as possible playing outside, but we talked about our dreams at the breakfast table most mornings. Every night, we'd climb on the couch and my mom would read to us, which, with seven kids, meant we got to listen to as many as fourteen stories before bedtime. My mom also had art books on the bookshelf from her college days, which my brothers and sisters and I were quite interested in because of the risqué and gory images they contained—warrior skeletons on horseback, saints who were beheaded or pierced by arrows, a naked woman at a picnic... An unintended positive consequence of our covert art book fascination was that, even as grade-schoolers, we could identify the artwork of painters such as Renoir, Rembrandt, da Vinci, van Gogh, Picasso, Degas, and Toulouse-Lautrec.

I have always had vivid dreams and astral experiences, and one of my worst nightmares ever was during this time of my life, when I dreamt I was trapped in a Seurat painting. The dream began with me sitting alone on some bleachers, watching a circus. As I looked around, I realized that all of the other spectators had an exaggerated and slightly sinister appearance. A feeling of impending doom came over me as I looked down in the ring, hoping to see someone who looked normal. It was then I realized the horse and circus performer were the ones depicted in Georges Seurat's *The Circus* and that I was stuck in a painting. My dream came to an ominous close as my perspective shifted from watching the circus to being an observer of my body, sitting alone and terrified as the observant me flew away from the scene backwards, leaving the real me completely deserted, even by myself. I don't remember exactly how old I was when I had this dream, but I couldn't have been more than eight. (I know this because we still lived in Ottawa, Minnesota, at the time, and we moved to the Black Hills of South Dakota a few months before I turned nine.)

I had my first precognitive dream when I was a first grader at St. Anne's Catholic elementary school in Le Sueur, Minnesota. I dreamt that our teacher, Mrs. McIntyre, asked me to pass out papers to all of my classmates. The next day, even though she had never before asked any student to do so, Mrs. McIntyre gave me a stack of papers to hand out. As

I walked up and down the aisles just like a teacher, I was so proud I could hardly stop smiling. (While writing this book, I discovered that some seventy years earlier, Annie McDonough, my great-grandma Maggie's younger sister, had attended St. Anne's. At the time, the late 1800s, it was a boarding school run by nuns. After their father died, one of Annie's older half-brothers felt she was not receiving sufficient supervision and arranged for her to go to school in the southern Minnesota town sixty miles away from St. Paul. My family ended up in the same small-town school through a completely unrelated set of circumstances. I think it's an odd coincidence, but I like the idea that, for a short time anyway, I attended the same school as Great-Grandma Maggie's little sister.)

Another unusual aspect of my life at this age was my belief that everyone died at night and came back to life every morning. I arrived at that conclusion because I had flying dreams at night in which I flew out of my body and around our neighborhood, over the fields and trees and rooftops. (I now believe that these were astral travel experiences, but that was a concept I didn't learn about until I was in my late teens.) In one of these flying dreams, I clearly remember looking down at the brown weeds poking up through ice-crusted snow and wondering why I wasn't cold. But when I mentioned to one of my younger siblings that we died each night, my mom corrected me. I was genuinely surprised when my mom said that we didn't die each night; we only died at the end of our life. She said I must have been dreaming that I was flying out of my body. Since I knew from church that our physical body was just a temporary home for our spirit, it didn't seem at all implausible to think of our spirits getting out and flying around every now and then.

This idea of spirits flying around eventually raised the question in my mind of whether ghosts could see you when you took a bath or went to the bathroom. I asked my mom about it, and she told me that spirits had more important things to do. Her answer did not allay my concerns, however, and I came up with an idea that I now view as an effective energetic shielding technique. In one of his sermons, our priest at church had talked about praying for people in the Iron Curtain countries. My mom told me that the phrase "Iron Curtain" was a way of saying that the people were not free to come and go as they pleased and were not free to express their beliefs about God or their government. I pictured the iron curtain as a heavy gray curtain that nothing could penetrate, like the curtain on the cabinet in which the communion wafers were kept at church but on a huge scale. So, whenever I wanted to shield myself from any spirits that might be around, I pictured a big slate-gray iron curtain encircling me and making me invisible.

The first overtly paranormal experience I remember from this time of my life was seeing yellow eyes watching me at night. They looked like animal eyes—elongated yellow eyes that glowed in the dark bedroom. I saw the yellow eyes quite often. I usually saw more than one pair of eyes, and I could see them whether my own eyes were open or closed. They would appear for a short time and then blink out, appearing again in a different spot but always on the edge of my bed or beyond—never any closer. I wasn't terrified, but I was scared because I knew there was no reasonable explanation for seeing eyes hovering around my room. I knew it couldn't be a dream, because I hadn't gone to sleep yet. I prayed to Jesus and my guardian angel to keep me safe. It never occurred to me to tell the eyes to go away, maybe because wishing they would go away didn't do any good. I shared a bed with my younger sister Betsy, but Betsy had the odd habit of sleeping with her eyes half open, so she wasn't much comfort. (When we were older, I asked Betsy if she had ever seen the yellow eyes at night, but she had not.)

When the yellow eyes appeared, I usually just closed my own eyes and told myself I was seeing things. It seemed less threatening to see yellow eyes in my mind's eye rather than hovering around my bed. I grew accustomed to the eyes that watched me at night, and since nothing bad ever happened when I saw them, I gradually became comfortable with the experience. Although I didn't know it at the time, it was an important lesson for me to learn that astral visions, even if they're weird or somewhat frightening, are usually just a form of information and not necessarily something to fear.

I've given a lot of thought over the years to what the yellow eyes might have signified. Although they looked wolflike, I don't think they represented a totem animal. I've had both dream visits and waking life visions of animal spirits and animal guides, and with one exception, the animal or bird has always appeared in complete physical form. I don't think the yellow eyes were associated with our house in southern Minnesota, since I saw them in other places where we lived throughout my childhood as well, although not as often. I've read that when people start meditating or developing their psychic abilities, their energy body, or aura, becomes brighter and may attract the attention of spirits and other astral beings. Maybe my intuitive abilities were starting to kick in at that age. At some subconscious level, unusual or intense eyes have been a theme in my life since I was young. When I was a child, I was constantly drawing eyes on my school papers and folders, and even now, if I doodle while on the phone or while otherwise distracted, I almost always draw either eyes or flowers. In both my dreams and shamanic journey experiences, I have seen characters with very strange eyes—eyes that have no whites, eyes that are twirling patterns, dazzlingly dark eyes that shine with magical power. One spirit I saw had no eyes—at least, not at first—just empty sockets. I've come to believe that the yellow eyes were a portent of my ability to see things that are hidden, the way many animals see well in the dark.

I've only seen the yellow eyes a handful of times as an adult, most recently within the last year. After all the unusual paranormal experiences I've had in my life, seeing the yellow eyes actually felt friendly and familiar, like a gift from the past.

Left to right: Aunt Mimi, Uncle Thomas, James, and
Grandma Dorrie in front of their St. Paul home, circa 1913.
Enterprising men would bring pony or goat carts such as this
around the city neighborhoods and charge a small fee for pictures.

Ireland is where strange tales begin...
Charles Haughey

❧❦

The Death Knock,
Bad-Luck Names, and
Other Irish Family Stories

When talking about the Irish side of my family, all stories begin or end with a party. From sit-down holiday dinners for more than seventy people, birthday celebrations held every month, graduation parties, anniversary soirees, and wedding and baby showers to card parties and weekly coffee meet-ups, we love to socialize. As my brother Dan says about our Irish relatives, "It's the party that never ends." Of course, pulling together when someone is ill or in need of help goes without saying, as are the bittersweet but comforting gatherings after one of our family members has died. My Irish great-grandma Maggie set the tone of unity, support, and celebration that is still a strong part of our family identity more than one hundred years later. (The image on the front cover of this book is of Maggie with her daughters Dorrie and Mimi.)

Maggie McDonough was my mom's maternal grandma. By the time I was around, in the 1960s, most of the bigger family gatherings had moved from Maggie's house to her daughters' houses. Great-Aunt Norah hosted Thanksgiving and Easter in St. Paul, and Grandma Dorrie had everyone down to her house in southern Minnesota for dinner on Christmas Day. These fancy dinner parties usually included some of the Irish friends and relatives that had been coming to family parties since the 1920s.

We still had smaller celebrations at Great-Grandma Maggie's house every now and then. I remember my great-grandma smiling at us kids from her chair while Big Uncle Thomas and Great-Aunt Mimi, who both lived with Great-Grandma, acted as hosts. Mimi was thin, with bright red hair and conservative but fashionable clothes. She was the first woman in the family to graduate from college, from the College of St. Thomas (now known as the University of St. Thomas). She worked as a librarian at the St. Paul Public Library. Mimi never married because she had fallen in love with a man who wasn't Catholic, and his parents had disapproved of the union. Mimi gave us kids books as gifts and took us to the ballet. Big Uncle Thomas was my godfather. He was loud, garrulous, and a generous spirit. He liked to drink, and he was a great storyteller. He gave us quarters and took us to Como Park, which had carnival rides and zoo animals. Thomas's wife Irene was very quiet, but she smiled a lot and had a wonderful sense of humor.

At the family parties, Big Uncle Thomas would bring in a grocery bag full of animal crackers and Cracker Jacks, a gift to us kids from Great-Grandma (see photo gallery at end of book). After thanking Great-Grandma, we'd make our way through the talking, laughing maze of grownups and head out to the porch to get down to the business of divvying up the goods. We always found out-of-the-way corners to play in at all of the main party houses—at my great-grandma's, it was the front porch.

I only knew my great-grandma Maggie when she was a very old woman. But I know some of the stories of her life, because both my mom and my grandma Dorrie spoke of her often. When they talked about Maggie, I could tell, even as a child, how much they loved and admired her. Their stories almost always started out with, "Great-Grandma had a very hard life, but she was a happy person ..."

My mom, my grandparents, and my mom's younger sister Veronica lived with my great-grandparents in St. Paul in the 1930s, while my grandpa finished law school. Grandma Dorrie worked as a buyer for the china department at the Emporium, a fancy department store in downtown St. Paul, so my great-grandma was the primary caretaker for my mom and Aunt Veronica when they were little. Also living in the four-bedroom house on the east side of St. Paul at that time were Great-Aunt Mimi, Big Uncle Thomas, Great-Aunt Nora, and Great-Aunt Nellie. Mimi's real name was Mary, but to everyone in our family born after 1934 she was Mimi, thanks to my one-year-old mom not being able to pronounce Mary. The name Mimi suited my great-aunt anyway, and it stuck.

I learned from my mom and grandma that Maggie loved to throw parties, play cards, and dance. Great-Grandma loved to sing, mostly songs from the Gay '90s. Several of the songs were very sad, such as "Hello, Central, Give Me Heaven, 'Cause My Mother's There" and "Poor Babes in the Woods," which my mom loved too—she said they both cried as Maggie sang them. Maggie also sang a song called "The Band Played On." (Decades later, I had a clairvoyant experience related to this song at one of my grade-school concert practices, covered in the "Bloody Mary and Ouija Boards" chapter.) Of course, Maggie sang Irish songs too, like "I'll Take You Home Again, Kathleen" and "The Minstrel Boy," a sad song about young men dying in a war. She sang while doing her housework—washing and ironing the clothes, doing the dishes, cleaning the house. My mom says she thinks singing cheered up my great-grandma.

Although she was taken out of school at age seven to help care for her younger siblings, Maggie was fluent in both Gaelic and English. She loved the outdoors, was a great rower and swimmer, and as a young woman, she used to swim across the Mississippi River. Maggie loved to cook and worked as one until she got married to Great-Grandpa Thomas. If people dropped by my great-grandparents' house unexpectedly, which they often did, Maggie could throw together a meal and still have the energy to roll up the rugs for a little dancing after dinner. My great-grandparents built a bar in their basement, painted white with a red ribbon trim, and hosted dances and poker games downstairs for their many guests. Our family likes to tell the story of how, during a blizzard, the streetcar that ran in front of my great-grandparents' house had to stop running. People came to my great-grandparents' door looking for a warm place to stay till the weather improved, and Thomas and Maggie let everyone in and gave them a drink. Eventually, they all moved into the basement to dance, turning everyone's bad weather luck into a party.

Maggie's father, Patrick, had lived in County Galway in Ireland. He owned a store and boat rental business near Carraroe on Galway Bay. Patrick had nine children with his first wife, Bridget. When Bridget died, Patrick got married again, to a woman named Mary, who was twenty years his junior. They came to America and soon helped all of Patrick's children from his first marriage emigrate, with the exception of his oldest daughter, who was married and wanted to stay in Ireland. In America, the six older half-brothers lived with my great-great-grandpa Patrick and turned their paychecks over to him. Maggie said her dad made all the clothes for the family. Maggie's two older half-sisters got married and set up their own households.

Maggie was my great-great-grandpa's first child with his second wife, Mary. Maggie had two younger sisters, Kate and Annie. According to my mom's sister Veronica, when Maggie was a child, she and her sister Kate would hide in the kitchen behind the stove and listen to the adults tell stories about the fairies, or "little people," and ghosts. Their dad told them about banshees, fearsome spirits whose keening and wailing presaged the death of someone in the family. He also told stories of leprechauns, the clever fairies who delight in outsmarting humans.

Maggie's mom died from complications of childbirth when Maggie was seven. On her deathbed, she said, "I'll come for you, Maggie." This was considered a very bad omen, as one of the Irish beliefs was that the last name spoken by a dying person revealed who would be next to die. My great-great-grandpa was terrified that the death coach, an old-fashioned spectral hearse that comes to collect the souls of the dead, was going to come for Maggie. He moved the four youngest kids into his room on a trundle bed to keep them safe at night from the banshees and the Irish death coach.

Maggie's father was in his mid-fifties when her mother died. He and seven-year-old Maggie tried to care for the baby and the two younger girls, who were three and two. (This is when Maggie was taken out of school.) Records are sketchy, but apparently the baby died only a month or so after her mom's death.

Another very sad story from Maggie's life is that four of her nine children died while they were young. Two died as infants; both were boys, and both were named John. One of the boys was a twin of Ethel, who died a few years later. In one terrible year, 1920, my great-grandma lost two children and her much-loved sister Annie. Annie, who lived with Maggie's family, died of tuberculosis. Maggie's five-year-old daughter Ethel died from scarlet fever, and her ten-year-old son James died of rheumatic fever. My mom's cousin Kay said that Annie got sick first, and she was so worried about someone else in the house getting tuberculosis that she prayed constantly. Great-Grandma felt that Annie's prayers had kept her family safe. After Annie died, Ethel and James got sick. My grandma Dorrie, only eleven or twelve years old herself, was at the bedside of her younger siblings when they died. According to my mom's cousin Bev, "After the scarlet fever and the deaths of Annie, Ethel, and James, (Great-)Grandpa moved the family because he believed the house was a sick, or sad, house, and he didn't want the family to live there." The house had actually been quarantined. After the quarantine was lifted, they moved a short distance away into the house that I call the Irish family homestead, because it was home to an ever-changing cast of Irish family members for the next eighty-five years.

Bev also told me that while James was sick, he told his mom that he saw St. Cecilia. (Cecilia was my great-grandma's middle name and one of her patron saints.) Great-Grandma asked James what St. Cecilia looked like, and he started to cry. When she asked him why he was crying,

James said, "Because you don't believe me." Bev said my great-grandma always felt bad about that. When I came across a memorial Maggie had written about James's death eighty years after she'd written it, I felt her heart-wrenching sorrow and despair leap off the scrap of paper before I'd even read the words: "My darling James died, Dec. 30, 1920, 7 AM." I am sensitive to energy, but I'd never felt anything like this shock of grief before. It was crushing. I said a prayer for both my great-grandma Maggie and James, and then for all of Maggie's children, thinking of the losses they had experienced in their lifetimes. I reminded myself that they've been reunited on the other side for many years now.

Maggie's son James's death was the second tragedy to befall a James in our family. Maggie's brother-in-law James (my great-grandpa Thomas's brother) had died unexpectedly at a young age, and Maggie and Thomas's son James had been named for this uncle. This led some of the older Irish relatives to declare James a bad-luck name for our family. (I'm not sure why the name John didn't fall into this category too, considering the two babies named John who had died.) Great-Aunt Mimi even made my mom's cousin Victor promise not to take the name James as a confirmation name or give the name to any son he might someday have.

My mom and grandma told me stories of my great-grandpa Thomas, too. Like Maggie, he was Irish and he had lost his mother at a young age. He was just ten years old when his mom died. Thomas completed high school at age sixteen and taught at a country school. He was very interested in politics and moved to St. Paul with the dream of going to law school. The family lore is that he lost his law-school money in a poker game shortly after arriving in the city. Thomas met Maggie when he was a customer at the restaurant where she cooked. He worked as a streetcar conductor when he was a young man, and sometimes he'd let Maggie ride for free.

Great-Grandpa liked to do magic tricks for his grandkids, like pulling nickels and quarters out from behind their ears. My mom remembers that he also loved to recite from memory the poem "Little Orphant Annie" by James Whitcomb Riley (see appendix III for the full text of this poem). The poem was outlandishly frightening—its most well-known line was "an' the Gobble-uns 'll git you, ef you Don't Watch Out!" My mom said the part of the poem that scared her most was a reference to two "big black things" that pulled a little girl through the ceiling:

They wuz two great big Black Things a-standin' by her side, an' they snatched her through the ceilin' 'fore she knowed what she's about!

Worst of all, my great-grandpa had a little door in his bedroom, about three feet high and two feet wide, which led to an attic crawl space. It was the perfect size for a goblin.

As a child, my mom also heard the true, tragic story of my great-grandma's friend, a nurse named Mrs. Brennan. Mrs. Brennan had seen her three-year-old daughter get struck and killed by a streetcar, and she had gone blind instantly. She never regained her sight for the rest of her life. When my mom told us this sad story, she told us what her grandma had told her—it was just an example of how things happen that we don't understand and can't explain.

My great-grandpa Thomas died in 1959, two years before I was born. Even though he died at a hospital, the Irish "death knock"—a loud, unexplained rap in the walls, heard when someone in the house has died—served as the announcement of his death to my great-grandma, who was waiting at home. I learned some of the details of my great-grandpa's death after Maggie's spirit came and had a sit-down visit with me a few years ago. I wrote about the visit in my first book, but one of the things my great-grandma told me was that she knew when her husband had died even though she "wasn't in the room with him." I asked my mom and Bev about some of the things Great-Grandma told me, and between them, they confirmed the accuracy of the information and filled me in on some new details. That's when I learned that, after the experience at her mother's deathbed, Maggie never again wanted to be in the room with a dying person. Bev, who is Norah's daughter and Maggie's granddaughter, said that she and Great-Grandma were at the Irish family homestead and most everyone else was at the hospital with

Great-Grandpa. Great-Grandma heard the death knock and told Bev that Great-Grandpa had died. A few minutes later, they got a call from the hospital confirming the news.

The other bit of Irish magic that marked my great-grandpa's passing was the little people stopping by to pay their respects. Maggie believed that the little people disguised themselves as rabbits when humans were around, and she would set out bread crusts and saucers of milk for them. When the family gathered at my great-grandparents' house after Great-Grandpa's funeral, an astonishing number of rabbits showed up. The rabbits came from the hill behind the house, ran across the yard in a large group, and disappeared into the woods across the street. This happened in the middle of the day. My great-grandparents had lived in that home for nearly forty years, and no one had ever seen anything like it.

The death knock was heard once again when my grandma's cousin Big Luke died. Big Luke was another relative who had lived at my great-grandma's house for many years. He had come over on a boat from Ireland at age five, alone; his only identification was a nametag around his neck. Big Luke was a gentle and kind man who had worked as a teacher until his retirement. He fought in WWI and had been shot in the head, but made a full recovery. At the family parties at my great-grandma's house when I was a child, he sat in a straight-backed chair by the porch door, smiling and greeting people as they passed, but not saying much.

Big Uncle Thomas's wife Irene told me about hearing the death knock when Big Luke died. Luke liked to spend time reading and had gone out to the porch with a book. Irene, Thomas, and my great-grandma were home at the time. Out of the blue, Irene and Thomas heard a loud knock. They went to the front door, but no one was there. Thomas went over to ask Luke if he'd heard or seen anything; Luke didn't respond. That's when Thomas realized that Luke was gone. Irene said they were going to try to keep the news from Maggie until they had it confirmed by a medical person, but when they came in from the porch, she already knew. She had heard the death knock, too.

One of my favorite Great-Grandma stories is the story of the fairies and the missing check. When Great-Aunt Norah's daughter Bev was a teenager, Norah called to tell her that her grandma Maggie had lost a check. Norah was at work, so Bev went over to help her grandma look for it. Maggie told Bev that she had already looked all over for the check and thought the fairies might have hidden it. Bev, who loved and respected Maggie, said, "Oh, Grandma, you don't really believe in fairies, do you?" Bev said it was the one time in her life that she felt she had offended her grandma. Bev felt bad when she realized that she had hurt her grandma's feelings, so she asked Maggie where the fairies might hide money. Together, they looked in the garden, the kitchen, and all around the house again. Bev said she had about given up when my great-grandma reached in her apron pocket and discovered the missing check. Bev was happy the check had been found and wasn't expecting Maggie's next comment: "How do you suppose the fairies got it into my pocket without me knowing?"

My mom told me that when the movie *Darby O'Gill and the Little People* first came out, Big Uncle Thomas brought Maggie to see it, hoping it would convince her that banshees and little people and the death coach were just superstitions. Instead, my great-grandma became more convinced than ever that they were real.

Throughout her life, my great-grandma prayed for her family each night, asking God's blessings for each person by name. In later years, she slept with a crucifix on her chest. When my great-grandma died, with many of her family members at her bedside, she called out to her mom. After all those years, her mother had kept her promise—she had come to take Maggie home.

B. T. and Tiny Gramma in front of their homestead
at the South Farm, Montana, circa 1921.

There seemed to be nothing to see; no fences, no
creeks or trees, no hills or fields. If there was a road,
I could not make it out in the faint starlight. There
was nothing but land: not a country at all, but
the material out of which countries are made.
Willa Cather, "My Antonia"

Montana Ghosts
and Pioneer Spirits:
My Dad's Cowboy Relatives

Every summer while I was growing up, my family would make
the twelve- to fourteen-hour trip out west to visit my grandma
Mae and grandpa Bernard Morgan. My dad grew up on the eastern prai-
rie of Montana, sometimes living in the country and sometimes in the
small town of Baker, depending on whether Grandpa Morgan was farming or doing in-town work, like repairing vehicles at a service garage
or selling farm machinery. My grandparents moved to a tiny western
North Dakota border town after my dad had left for college and lived
there for the rest of their lives, so that's the place that is familiar to me.
We would visit all the Montana relatives when we were there, of course,
going back and forth between everyone's places.

I loved the big sky of Montana, the buttes, and the stark landscape
that went on as far as the eye could see, occasionally broken up by tall
cottonwood trees or small, crooked rivers and creeks. Montana had
fields and pastures, but they didn't look like the ones back in Minnesota.
Towns and houses were few and far between. A railroad track ran along
the highway for hours and hours, coming right through Grandma and

Grandpa's town before heading farther west through Montana, Idaho, and Washington State, all the way to the Pacific Ocean.

One of my favorite North Dakota memories is of my parents waking us kids up in the early hours of the morning as we drove past my Uncle Jim's place in the country, which meant we'd be arriving at Grandma and Grandpa Morgan's house a few minutes later. (When we were little, we left Minnesota at suppertime and my dad drove all night, so we kids would be asleep for most of the trip. This was in the days before car seats, so my mom would hold whoever was the baby on her lap the entire time.) When we got to town, we'd turn left at the main intersection and go down a few blocks to my grandparents' house at the end of town.

Because we generally saw our Montana grandparents only once a year, we kids were always shy when we first arrived. Grandpa Morgan was a hardworking and laconic Montana farmer, but as a grandpa he was a teddy bear, a kind man who gave bear hugs. Whenever we saw our grandpa, he'd reach out with a smile and say, "Give us a love," and then he'd give us a big hug. We'd feel much more comfortable after a hug and kiss from him. Grandma Morgan was a schoolteacher who still taught classes in the 1960s and '70s. The school at which she taught was so small, she usually taught two entire grades at a time; one year, she had only nine kids in her class. Grandma Morgan was kind of a cowgirl grandma—sometimes she said damn and once she saved me and my siblings and cousins from a big rattlesnake that had slithered under the front porch. (When she came out to take a look at it, she told us it was actually a bull snake, but to make us feel better, she said bull snakes and rattlers looked a lot alike.) Grandma Morgan also had an affectionate side. She'd say, "Guess what time it is?" And, since she had taught us the answer, we would reply, "Half-past kissing time—time to kiss again!"

When we visited our Montana relatives, we did cowboy things like going to the Fourth of July rodeo in town or watching from outside the corral as our grandpa, my dad, and uncles branded cows. Even my aunt Sister, who was a nurse, was part of the branding process, giving each cow an antibiotic shot. Sister, who is also a nun in the Catholic order

Sisters of the Charity of Leavenworth, or SCL, wore a big apron over her black dress and a simple white veil for the occasion.

Grandma and Grandpa Morgan's house had lots of interesting places to explore and things to do. For a while, they had an antique player piano, and I remember putting a musty paper roll in the piano and pretending to play "Winchester Cathedral" over and over. We also loved looking at the sparkly and colorful costume jewelry that my grandma kept on her dressing table. My mom had a pair of earrings made from real rattle-snake tails that my dad had made for her when they were first married, but my grandma apparently didn't own a pair herself, even though she lived in rattlesnake country.

My grandparents' house had a spooky basement with a steep and narrow enclosed staircase. The rise behind the third or fourth step was missing, creating a black hole that you had to walk in front of each time you went into the old basement, which we didn't do very often. The house was heated with an "octopus" furnace, a huge, loud monster that was intimidating even when it wasn't running. Outside, right next to the house, was an empty cistern about twelve feet deep and fifteen feet in diameter. We were told to be careful around it, but I do remember one of my cousins goofing around and falling in. He wasn't hurt (it was made of cement, but my grandpa kept a deep pile of leaves in the bottom just in case someone fell in), and it definitely earned my cousin extra coolness points with the rest of us.

Grandpa Morgan, as a child, had lived in a homestead shack in South Dakota, just like Laura Ingalls Wilder. They had to set their bed frame posts in kerosene to keep the bed bugs from climbing up. My dad said the bed bugs outsmarted them by climbing up to the ceiling and dropping into the beds. Grandma Morgan, who had grown up in the small Minnesota town that my grandma and grandpa Haraldson had moved to in the late 1930s, moved out to Montana as a young woman to teach at a one-room country school. She roomed at my great-grandparents' house, which is how she and my grandpa met and fell in love. It took my grandpa a while to propose, and when he finally asked my grandma to marry him, it was on April Fool's Day. My grandpa and his brothers had a reputation for pulling pranks, and it took my grandma a week to decide that the proposal was sincere and he wasn't pulling her leg. When Grandma and Grandpa Morgan first got married in 1930, they lived in an abandoned homestead shack in eastern Montana. In time, a bigger and better homestead shack was abandoned, and they moved into that.

Grandpa Morgan had a strong sense of intuition that was described in our family as Grandpa just "knowing things." He didn't really talk about it; it was just part of his life. My grandpa wasn't particularly superstitious or religious—he was just "in tune." Grandpa Morgan, who wasn't Catholic, didn't go to church until he was older. My aunt Sister said that when they were growing up, Grandma Morgan made them say a prayer for my grandpa's conversion to Catholicism every Good Friday between 1 and 3 PM. Apparently, the prayers worked, because according to my dad:

Grandpa was baptized in about 1947 or '48 by Father Ciabattone, who was the Italian priest in Baker for many years. As Father C. got older, he was not able to drive, so my folks volunteered to drive him to his mission churches—Ekalaka, Plevna, Mildred, Webster, and others. The driver was generally me, as I had a license—Larry did not have his license yet—it was not proper for ladies to drive priests around, I guess. So when I couldn't or wouldn't drive, it was up to my dad. My dad had a lot of respect for Father C., and Father C. thought my dad was probably the best Christian he ever met, and the two got along great. These trips were half-day ventures and provided a lot of time for discussion. When Father C. finally retired, he was going back to Italy. He told my dad he had one last favor he would like to ask before he went, and that would be to baptize him, so my dad agreed. From then on, Grandpa was a regular churchgoer, probably more so than any of the rest of us. Prior to this, he seldom if ever went to church except for his mother's funeral.

My dad also told me the story of how my grandparents were out driving on the highway one day. They waved as they passed their neighbor, who was in his vehicle going the opposite way. After a few minutes of traveling, my grandpa said, "We have to turn around." He knew that the neighbor they had just passed had been in an accident and needed help. My grandparents turned around and drove the way they had come and found the neighbor had gone into the ditch, which was really steep. They helped him get his car back on the road and went on their way.

My uncle Jim said that when he was a teenager, my grandpa somehow knew that he had skipped classes to go to a big two-day music festival, Zip to Zap, in the little town of Zap. The outdoor concert was North Dakota's version of Woodstock and took place at the same time. Jim said he and his buddies were picked up at the concert and were some of the first concertgoers brought to jail in Bismarck for underage drinking. At the jail, Jim said the police officers took away their beer and told them to go home.

Jim, who still lives in western North Dakota, is my dad's youngest brother. Jim, a former chief of police, is a member of the volunteer fire department (made up of, according to Jim, "however many people show up") and has a repair shop where he fixes just about any kind of vehicle that breaks down (see photo gallery). He also raises sheep. His wife, Vernice, runs the town café.

Jim is a great storyteller who, among other things, owned a pet monkey that he became a lot less fond of when he discovered it peeing on his pancake one day. Jim was the original owner of our albino horse Trigger. Jim had gotten Trigger in the 1950s and used to do tricks with him, such as running up behind Trigger and jumping on his back while Trigger stood still (and probably kept eating grass). Jim gave Trigger to my brother Thomas sometime in the sixties. We kept Trigger until the midseventies, when Jim and Vernice had kids of their own. Then Thomas gave Trigger back to Jim so his kids could enjoy him, too. After bringing a lot of happiness to three generations of kids in our family, Trigger died peacefully out in his home turf of North Dakota.

Both my uncle Jim and his wife, Vernice, had near-death experiences. Vernice had an aneurysm, and it was touch and go for a while. Along with all of us in the family, their entire cmmunity was praying for her safe recovery. Jim said that when someone needs help, the people in their small town pull together and everyone pitches in. Vernice, who made a complete recovery, does not have any memory of seeing angels or lights or even of being in the hospital, although she was there for two weeks.

Jim had a near-death experience when he was electrocuted while working at a construction site. A boom hit a power line, and Jim heard a hum like the sound a transformer makes. He realized what was happening and yelled at the guy next to him to get away, so he wouldn't get electrocuted too. Jim said the last thing he remembers before losing consciousness was hoping that someone at the job site knew CPR. He saw a bright light at the end of a tunnel, and "a bunch" of hooded beings in white robes at the far end of the tunnel. Then he heard a voice say, "He's not ready. Send him back." And Jim said just like that, he got sent back like an undercooked steak at a restaurant. The next thing he knew, a big, burly guy was "shaking the sh** out" of him. Jim asked his coworkers which one of them had given him CPR. One of the guys answered, "No one, 'cause we thought you were dead."

Jim told them thanks a lot and called them a cuss word. (He later learned from a doctor that the force with which he hit the ground probably restarted his heart.) But he had other things to deal with at that moment, because the electrical charge had blown out through the bottom of his foot, and once he got his boot off, he discovered his sock was still smoldering. Jim has not experienced any of the common aftereffects of a near-death experience such as clairvoyance or healing abilities, but he was told by an energy healer (who didn't know anything about him or his life) that his polarities were reversed.

When I was a teenager, my grandpa Morgan got sick with ulcers and lymphoma. He had already beaten cancer once before in his life, back in the 1930s, when he had gotten lip cancer from smoking. In those days, cigarettes had no filters. My grandpa worked as a mechanic at the time and his hands were usually covered with grease, so instead of touching the cigarettes, he would let them dangle on his lip till they burned his mouth. My grandpa's Montana doctor had sent him to a clinic in Savannah, Missouri, for a natural remedy for the lip cancer. The treatment consisted of a poultice being applied to my grandpa's mouth where the tumor was, and then a bandage put over it. After three weeks or so of daily treatments, the tumor came out one day, stuck on the bandage. Although my grandpa had a notch on his lip where the tumor had been, the remedy did take care of the cancer. According to my dad:

> I was about five or six at the time, and I remember my dad getting on the Greyhound bus in Baker and being gone three or four weeks. My mother and Francis R. ran the Willard store while he was gone. When Grandpa came back, he had a notch in his lower lip where a couple of teeth showed through. It eventually filled in a little, but he always had the scar.
>
> I do not know what eventually happened to the Savannah clinic, but we would get a book from them every year for five or six years with the name, address, and type of cancer they had cured. I would always look up Dad's name in the book. When we would talk about it in later years, Grandpa maintained the "established medical profession" shut them down because they had a cure that the "profession" could not control or profit from.

In the 1970s, when he got cancer again, my grandpa went to the Denver hospital where Sister was a nurse. He went through chemotherapy treatments in Denver and back home in Montana. He kept on working with my uncle Jim for as long as he could. My dad told me that Grandpa was the kind of man who would want to die with his boots on, working outside, doing the things he loved to do. He wouldn't want to spend time in a hospital, even if it meant he might live a little longer. My grandma Morgan took care of Grandpa at home, in the same room where she had taken care of her dad, Great-Grandpa Schultz, a little more than a decade earlier when he died. Sister came up to stay with my grandparents when my grandpa needed more help at the end. Grandpa Morgan was in a coma for the last few weeks of his life, but on his seventy-fifth birthday, he woke up. He passed away shortly after telling my grandma he loved her.

My grandpa's spirit paid a visit to my grandma one afternoon, a few months after he died. Grandma had lain down for a nap. She thought she heard someone come in the back door, just like my grandpa used to do. She waited to see if Uncle Jim, Aunt Vernice, or any of their kids would come in. No one did, so she thought she must have imagined the sound of the door opening. Then she felt my grandpa come in the room. He lay down on the bed beside her and put his arms around her. She wondered if she was having a vivid dream or possibly losing her mind, then she heard Grandpa say, "Don't investigate, just appreciate"—which sounded just like something my grandpa would say.

Five years later, Grandma Morgan died. After retiring, she had started a senior citizen's center in their small town and kept busy with church activities, substitute teaching, and spending time with Jim's family, our other Montana relatives, and her friends. Although my grandma had lived a long life and remained independent to the end of her life, it was very sad to go to her funeral. Along with the sadness of Grandma being gone, I knew that her passing marked the end of an era. I wondered how often we would get back to Montana and spend time with our cowboy cousins. Happily for our family, we have established a tradition of coming together for big family reunions every other year or so.

. . . . . .

The stories of my Montana and pioneer great-grandparents I heard bits and pieces of occasionally while I was growing up, but my uncle Larry collected the family histories and photographs into genealogy books that are informative and filled with great stories. My grandpa Morgan's maternal grandparents were Tiny Gramma (whose parents were born in Scotland) and B. T. McClain, a second-generation American whose grandfather had emigrated from Ireland. Tiny Gramma had bright red hair when she was young and was only five feet tall. When she was fifteen years old and B. T. was twenty-two, he met her on his way up to Canada on a military assignment. Tiny Gramma and her family lived in northern Minnesota, and according to family lore, B. T. told Tiny Gramma (whose name was Mary Ann), "Little girl, I'll be back to pick you up!"

B. T. did come back for Tiny Gramma after he completed his stint with the military, and they were married for fifty-four years, from 1871 to 1925, making a life of homesteading and farming. They did well enough that eventually they were able to have a state-of-the-art house built, complete with indoor plumbing fixtures, including a bathtub and a toilet. Unfortunately, the property didn't have a septic system, so they were never able to actually use the bathroom. Their house also had carbide lights, a type of lighting that used explosive gas as a main component and was, according to my dad, "not the safest."

Tiny Gramma was a midwife for all of her adult life. She lived to be ninety-eight years old and was spry and active to the end. Her daughter Dana carried on her mother's natural-healing legacy, offering Denver mudpack treatments for a variety of ailments. (My dad said the mudpack treatments involved "putting warm mud in a dishtowel and wrapping it around [the ailing person's] chest.") B. T., who never learned to drive a car, would hitch up a horse and buggy (called a rig) even in his later years. According to my uncle Larry, at age eighty, Great-Great-Grandpa B. T. McClain "passed on in a very stately manner. He sang hymns on his deathbed, namely 'Beulah Land,' 'Old Rugged Cross,' and 'Nearer My God to Thee.'"

B. T. and Tiny Gramma's daughter Cora married my great-grandpa David Morgan. David's father had been the third son of an Englishman. The custom in England at that time decreed that the oldest son be named Thomas, the second son be named John, and the third son, Edward. The eldest son inherited all the property, while any other sons were taught a trade, joined the military, or went to sea. Great-Grandpa David Morgan's father was born on the feast day of St. David, so his parents broke with tradition and named him David instead of Edward, perhaps establishing a theme of independent thinking that was to mark his life. (My dad said this naming convention stopped with that generation, but I believe that the energetic pattern of the tradition may have taken a while to fade away. My dad was unaware of the tradition when my older brother Thomas was born, yet my parents chose the "first son" family name for him. Also, according to my dad, who was the oldest son of Grandma and Grandpa Morgan:

> When I was about six, I wanted to change my name to Tom, without being aware of the tradition. I ordered a pencil box from an ad in the funny papers where you could have your name on the pencils, so I had three Tom Morgan pencils for a while. I didn't want to sharpen them past the Tom Morgan name, so they lasted quite a while.

As a young man, Great-Great-Grandpa David left England to take his chances in North America. He and his family of twelve moved from Canada to a homestead in South Dakota in the late 1800s. His son, David Morgan, was a bit of a wheeler-dealer and a great conversationalist who loved to fish and apparently never really took to being a farmer. Great-Grandpa David Morgan never learned to drive an automobile, but in his midlife years, he became completely stuck on the idea of developing a perpetual motion machine. According to my uncle Larry, "He had bicycle wheels, ball bearings, belts, pulleys, and vials of mercury all over the place." And despite the efforts of his four sons to convince him otherwise, Great-Grandpa Morgan never gave up on his dream.

When I spoke with psychic Patrick Mathews six or seven years ago, my grandpa Morgan's spirit came through. He told Patrick to let me know the family "is all together on the other side." I didn't know what my grandpa was referring to, but when I asked my mom, she said there had been some sort of falling out over a family business venture in the 1930s or '40s. In Larry's genealogy book, I read that Tiny Gramma had sent a letter to one of the relatives saying she was sorry to hear that everything had "gone to smack." So, it's good to know that the feuding ended and the family is united in the spirit realm.

My grandma Mae Morgan, whose maiden name was Schultz, had grown up in the same small southern Minnesota town that my mom and her family moved to in the late 1930s. Grandma Mae's niece Judith was my mom's best friend in school, and that's how my mom met my dad years later.

In 1861, my great-grandpa Schultz's dad ran away to join the army, hitchhiking from Mankato to Fort Snelling. He was twelve years old at the time. His mom had died, and his dad had farmed out all of the kids (which basically meant sending them to earn their keep by working on neighboring farms) and become a soldier. Great-Great-Grandpa didn't like being a farm hand, and he wanted to be with his dad. So he enlisted in the army as a drummer boy. After the war was over, the regiment went to Washington, D.C., where my great-great-grandpa saw President Lincoln in person. In a newspaper interview when he was an old man, Great-Great-Grandpa Schultz described Lincoln as someone who "appeared careworn, but who looked very kind and ready to help anyone."

Great-Great-Grandpa Schultz must have been a little bit psychic, because he foretold who his son was going to marry. According to a story that my great-grandma Edith Schultz told her daughter Clara, when she (Great-Grandma Schultz) was seventeen, she and her cousin were playing checkers on a winter night during a blizzard. Her brother Henry came bursting in the house to tell them a team of horses had fallen on the hill at the Schultz homestead across the field. Great-Grandma Edith and her cousin put on their coats and boots and ran outside with Henry. They could see that the horses were "lathered in their struggle to regain their footing." The Schultz family had made the move from Wisconsin to southern Minnesota, and their wagon was packed with all of their household belongings. A woman and three young girls stood shivering on the roadside, while the father and a teenage boy struggled to get the horses up. The father straightened up, brushed the icicles off his "walrus-like" moustache, and stopped to catch his breath for a moment. Then he caught sight of my great-grandma and her cousin across the road and, in the midst of the blizzard and the downed horses and the neighbors who had gathered around, he said to his son, "Willie, that black-haired girl is the one you are going to marry." And my great-grandma Edith and William Schultz did marry nine years later. Ironically, my great-great-grandpa, the former drummer boy who made the prediction, didn't attend the wedding. He didn't approve of the marriage since his family was Lutheran and my great-grandma Edith was Catholic.

We used to go visit Great-Grandma and Great-Grandpa Schultz when I was a kid. (See photo gallery for pictures of Great-Grandma and Great-Grandpa Schultz.) I was always a little intimidated by their quiet little house and their old-fashioned ways. They were hardworking and good people, but Great-Grandma seemed a little stern and Great-Grandpa was quiet, with a gaze that was startling in its intensity. Great-Grandma was very short and wore dark dresses and aprons all the time. She had long hair, like a kid, which she kept braided and tied on top of her head.

I had heard a story on one of our Montana visits that, decades earlier, Great-Grandma Schultz had a terrible dream about a plane crash and was so upset by it that she couldn't go to church the next morning. Great-Grandma had dreamt that a plane had crashed into their neighbor's yard. The neighbors were good friends of their family—the mom was my Great-Aunt Clara's godmother, and the daughter, Sally Mae, was Clara's friend the whole time they were growing up. In Great-Grandma's dream, Sally Mae was there when the plane crashed, and Great-Grandma saw someone covering her with a sheet. The next day in church, my Great-Grandpa learned that Sally Mae and her baby had perished in a plane crash the day before. From then on, I worried that Great-Grandma Schultz could read my mind when we were at their house for visits, so I tried to think only nice thoughts. It was a lot of work.

Great-Grandma Schultz's mother, Great-Great-Grandma Wieland, had premonitions, too. Her son Henry moved in with her after his father died. Great-Uncle Henry was a kind man with many friends, but he never married. (See photo gallery for photos of Great-Great-Grandma Wieland and Great-Uncle Harry.) He had been injured as a child when he fell off a horse. As a result, one of his legs was four to six inches shorter than the other leg, and he had to wear a special shoe. Henry's brother Bill was one of my relatives (there were at least three or four) who had a hard time making the transition from horses to automobiles.

When he got his first car, he drove it into the garage but forgot how to stop it, so he just yelled, "Whoa, whoa."

Henry preceded his mother in death. Great-Aunt Clara wrote for our family genealogy book that Great-Great-Grandma Wieland knew before she climbed the narrow stairway to Henry's room that he had died, because the night before she had "felt someone's hands feeling alongside the quilt of her bed." Another story Clara shared about Great-Great-Grandma Wieland was that whenever one of her children died, a star fell across their house. Great-Great-Grandma Wieland had thirteen kids, but only eight lived to adulthood. She lost five children, all under the age of two, in a five-year period. The children died from diptheria and whooping cough. Despite her many losses and hardships, Grandma Wieland was always in good health, right to the end of her life. At age eighty-seven, she came down with pneumonia and seemed "resolved to die." Again from Clara's reminisces:

> (Great-Great-Grandma Wieland) had a good appetite and ate a meal of sauerkraut and pork the night before she took to her bed, which was a Sunday. She told (Great-Grandma Schultz) what dress she wanted to be buried in, refused to eat the custard that I (Clara) made for her (taking one look at it and saying, "What's that?").

On her deathbed, Great-Great-Grandma Wieland fixed her own hair, which, like Great-Grandma Schultz, she wore in two braids, crossed over the top of her head and tied with a string. (Clara had been trying to fix her grandma's hair but was taking too long.) One family member tried to give her a rosary, others tried to get her to agree to let a minister come by, but Great-Great-Grandma said she didn't want either one. She died two days after taking to her bed, on May 31, 1932.

It's not written down anyplace and I haven't heard anyone tell the story, but I hope that, on the night she died, one more star fell over the house for Great-Great-Grandma Wieland.

My mom and siblings and me at the bunkhouse, Mountain Ranch,
South Dakota, circa 1969. Left to right: Iris (on horse), Maggie,
me, Randall, Betsy, my mom, Dan, and Thomas (on horse).

And when, on the still cold nights, he
pointed his nose at a star and howled long
and wolflike, it was his ancestors, dead and
dust, pointing nose at star and howling down
through the centuries and through him.
Jack London, *"The Call of the Wild"*

Spirit Land:
Stories from
the Black Hills

In 1969, my dad got a job managing a sand-mining plant in the tiny town of Pringle, South Dakota. My dad had gone out to South Dakota to check it out and sent back a letter naming some aspect of the Black Hills that he thought would appeal to each of us. I still remember that for me, he wrote, "Annie will like the wildflowers here." My dad built a frame for the bed of his pickup truck, and our horse Trigger and dogs Duke and Duchess rode out to South Dakota in the back of the pickup. A couple of my siblings rode out to our new home in the truck with my dad, while my mom drove the station wagon with the rest of us kids and our cats, who made the trip in a cat taxi made from two laundry baskets tied together.

In the Black Hills, we moved into a two-bedroom pink house that had a tin roof. It was the bunkhouse of a thousand-acre ranch called Mountain Ranch. My three sisters and I shared one bedroom, my parents had the other, and my three brothers slept on the screened porch on a triple bunk bed my dad had built out of PVC pipe and plywood. The house had no phone and no furnace, just a propane stove in the living room.

We had to haul our water from a well. Once our water tasted really bad and my mom had to boil it before we could use it for drinking or cooking. My dad investigated and discovered a bunch of dead squirrels in our cistern.

Although it must have been daunting for my mom to live in a place so rustic, for us kids, Mountain Ranch was a tremendously fun adventure. We felt like pioneers, and our house was deluxe compared to houses we visited. When we went to see some friends who were in the process of building their new house, someone had to use the bathroom. When my mom asked where the bathroom was, our friends pointed to an empty coffee can.

Lloyd and Marla, the ranchers who owned Mountain Ranch, told my dad that we could ride any of the horses that they kept at the ranch. The ranch had a bunch of outbuildings and, of course, a lot of land to explore. We were told to stay away from the root cellar and to be careful by the water cistern. Because there were rattlesnakes and sidewinders on the property, we had to wear cowboy boots when we were outside. We older kids also had to carry a jackknife with us. My dad taught us what to do if we saw a snake and also what to do if one of us was bitten by a rattlesnake. He said to make two small cuts around the bite, suck the venom out, and spit it on the ground. Then we were supposed to run for help. We never did see a snake at Mountain Ranch, although we did see sidewinder tracks in the sandy driveway when we made our nearly mile-long trek to get the mail, water canteens and sandwiches in tow. The scariest creature we encountered at Mountain Ranch was a huge spider on our bedroom wall that was the color of dust and had a body the size and texture of a milkweed pod.

My brothers and sisters and I spent the summer mostly outside, riding the horses, playing pioneer games, and prospecting for gold in the sandy driveway using an old pie pan. We discovered an injured magpie and nursed it back to health. Our dad told us magpies could learn to talk, and so we often went into the old building where we kept the bird and tried desperately to get it to say our names, hello, hi, or anything at all. The magpie recovered after a few weeks and flew away one day without saying a word.

My dad occasionally hunted on our land, shooting deer for us to eat. He shot a wild turkey for our first and last Thanksgiving in the house, right before we moved to town. And my mom and dad joined a square-dancing club while we lived at Mountain Ranch. They would bring my youngest siblings over to Lloyd and Marla's. My mom's dress was blue and white, with sparkly silver rickrack trim. My dad wore a new cowboy hat and a nice Western shirt. They taught us the square-dance moves they learned, and we had square dances and polkas in our living room to the music of the Chmielewski Funtime Band. We also said the rosary as a family while living at Mountain Ranch. I liked the drama and ritual of saying the rosary together, and I felt like I was getting a leg up on religion, which was good, as I would be making my first communion in the next school year. None of us experienced any ghostly activity at Mountain Ranch, but I did have occasional moments of luminescent happiness that I have been able to return to throughout my life, a transcendent awareness of how magical and good life is. I remember being struck by how cool it was to be exactly where I was in the world and in my life, with my family and our animals and the land. I was keenly aware of how sad it would be when things changed. We knew that we would have to leave Mountain Ranch and move into town before winter, and that probably made our summer there more poignant.

When school started that fall, we older kids rode into Pringle with our dad and then caught the school bus to Custer, which was the nearest town that had a school. There were five of us kids piled in the pickup truck, with the two youngest kids sitting on the laps of the older kids. We stayed at Mountain Ranch until right after Thanksgiving, then moved to Custer.

All of us in my family agree that the Black Hills have a spiritual power that is palpable. Over the last thirty years, any of us who have gone out to the Black Hills have made the pilgrimage to Mountain Ranch. In the early 1980s, I was still married to John, Molly and Jack's dad, and we vacationed in the Black Hills. When we stopped at Mountain Ranch, a man carrying a shotgun met us in the driveway. He got a lot friendlier when we told him that I had lived in the house a decade earlier and even let us take a few pictures. I was dismayed to see a sewer pipe sticking straight out the bathroom window that apparently emptied into the driveway. But I didn't mention that to the man with the gun.

My brother Thomas made a stop at Mountain Ranch on a long road trip he took after finishing pharmacy school in the summer of 1986. He stopped in to see Marla, and she mentioned that some cult people were living in the area. She told Thomas he could drive up to Mountain Ranch if he liked, as no one was living there. He said he remembers the driveway being very rutted and rough, and it was a bit of a struggle even for the big Catalina, a beast of a car that my dad had gotten at a police auction. According to Thomas:

> The house looked rough—weeds grown up everywhere, and the door off the hinges. It was really hot and still, and I remember a lot of mosquitoes or gnats buzzing around, so it was kind of quiet and glum. There were no other vehicles parked anywhere. As I walked into the old house and entered the living room, right in the center of the floor I saw two new-looking sleeping bags side by side—turned open like someone had just jumped out of them. I never saw anyone and am not sure if anyone saw me. I decided not to stay long after that! It had a much different feel than I had for it in my memories—even the photos I took from the stop turned out depressed and mismatched. Guess I had in mind nostalgic and rustic and just found neglected and abandoned—perhaps not completely abandoned! I have such great memories of that summer we lived there (other than the longest week ever of church school in Pringle).

In 2006, my mom and dad, my son Jack, and I were out in the Black Hills to consult with a natural healer. When we finally found Mountain Ranch, it was almost unrecognizable, but in a good way, thankfully.

There had been a lot of rain that spring, and everything was greener than it had ever been when we lived there. The land had been divvied up, but not too much. There were a few more rustic houses in what had been our thousand-acre paradise, but they looked like they belonged there. We drove by Lloyd and Marla's old place and were surprised and delighted to find Marla out watering her flowers. She must have been in her eighties by then. She remembered my mom and dad and the square dancing. She told us Lloyd had passed away. My dad asked her if she ran her place all by herself, and she said, "Oh, all I've got now is a few cows, sheep, goats, chickens, cats, and a dog." Weirdly, at the time, Warren Jeffs, the polygamist sect leader, had bought up a bunch of land behind Marla's house. She told us the authorities had been out to talk to her, but she was unwilling to move at this point in her life. My dad asked her if she was worried, and she laughed and said, "Naw—what would they want with an old lady like me?" She said she believed that it would all work out all right. We were relieved when the FBI apprehended Jeffs in Las Vegas a few months later.

When we moved from Mountain Ranch into town, we had looked at a few unusual places before finding the house we bought in Custer. I love it that my mom and dad were open to nontraditional possibilities, like considering buying a one-room country schoolhouse for us to live in. My mom loved the schoolhouse because it had a loft with wooden steps leading up to it and a big blackboard on one wall. My dad decided it needed too much work to turn it into usable home space for our family of nine. Another house we looked at was an abandoned Victorian mansion at an intersection on Custer's main street. My parents decided the location was too busy, so we kept looking. The people who did buy the mansion turned it into a haunted museum of terror, called Monster Mansion, which we toured. I got so scared during the tour I literally froze at the top of the staircase and could not move. The actor propped against the wall at the bottom of the steps had to take off his mask before I could come down the stairs and run past him. The house my parents ended up buying was on the edge of a Native American reservation. It had a circular driveway with a picnic area inside a teardrop-shaped fence. Inside the fence, someone had built a hexagonal picnic table around a pine tree. The driveway looked like a magical road. It had flakes of mica and both rose and white quartz that sparkled in the sunlight. My dad built an addition for the house and, using painted two-by-fours, he extended the roofline in a way that framed some pine trees and incorporated them right into our house design. Behind our house were pine tree woods with the black boulders for which South Dakota is known. In our horse pasture, there was a big gray rock that we called Elephant Rock. The small boulder beside it was Baby Elephant Rock. Back behind our house was a maze of boulders that created the effect of many rooms and hallways with dried pine-needle floors. That was Castle Rock. My brothers and sisters and I would ride our bikes to nearby French Creek, a small, hidden-away stream, and have picnic lunches. I believe the drama and beauty of the Black Hills and the freedom we had as kids to explore our surroundings opened me up and attuned me to the natural world.

The really creepy thing about our house in Custer was that there were spiders everywhere—in the sink, in the tub, on the walls, and on the ceilings. My dad said it was because the house didn't have a basement, only a crawl space. Before my dad put the addition on the house, Iris, Betsy, Maggie, and I shared a bedroom. We three younger sisters had a triple bunk bed, and as the oldest, I had the top bunk, which was only about a foot and a half away from the ceiling. One morning, I woke up to a big black spider right above my face. I ducked down under the covers and called for help, but no one heard me. I finally had to work myself down to the far end of my bed while still under my blanket and escape that way.

I usually didn't feel scared at our house in Custer, although it is where I had the first really dramatic ghost encounter of my life. I was home alone because I was sick and had stayed home from school. My mom had gone into town to pick up my brothers and sisters. I was dozing in my mom and dad's bed when I heard noises that sounded like a big party was going on—talking and laughter, glasses clinking, the sounds of people moving around. I got scared, since I was pretty sure I was home alone, so there was no reason for the noises I was hearing. I got out of bed, but when I tried to open the bedroom door, it wouldn't open. I went back to bed for a minute, then it occurred to me that maybe my mom had gotten home and everyone was in the kitchen, having an after-school snack without me. I jumped out of bed, and this time, my parent's bedroom door opened easily. I walked past the bathroom and through the utility room, coming in the back way to join everyone in the kitchen, but when I opened the door, the kitchen was empty and silent. My stomach dropped. Just an instant before, it had sounded like there was a roomful of people on the other side of the door. I called out, "Mom?" There was no answer. Now really scared, I walked into our living room, which was sunny and bright at that time of day. I sat on the couch, looking all around me as I said the only prayer I could think of, "Jesus Loves Me." There was a big picture window in our living room, from floor to ceiling, and in the afternoon, you could see the dust motes floating in the bright sunshine. I started watching the dust particles when I noticed something odd happening—the specks of dust were beginning to shake and shimmer and take a human form. At first, I thought it might be my guardian angel or Jesus coming to help me, but then I realized the shimmering figure looked like a man standing in the air about a foot above the ground. I ran outside and held on to our newest dog, Lobo, until my mom got home. Then I started to cry. I never saw or heard anything else that seemed ghostly at our house, but with our big family, I was probably never alone there either.

Iris saw a ghost at our house in Custer too, even before I did. She had gotten up early, while it was still dark, to try to finish a paper that was due that day. She was going to work at the kitchen table and turned on a light in the living room as she walked through. She didn't turn on the kitchen light right away, though there was light in the table area shining through the doorway from the living room. She said she was still pretty sleepy, so the first thing she did was lie down on the bench and shut her eyes for a few minutes. (My dad made our kitchen table, and instead of chairs, he made long benches to go with it.) When Iris opened her eyes, she saw a large black cat with glowing orange eyes sitting under the table, about a foot and a half from her face, looking at her. She said that she and the cat stared at each other for three or four seconds, then it vanished. It didn't seem like she was dreaming, because seeing the cat jolted her into a state of high alertness, and the cat was still very vividly there. Iris decided then to go back to bed. She said that, although the cat didn't seem to have any threatening intentions, she didn't feel like staying in the kitchen alone. Iris can't remember the outcome of not getting her homework done.

My youngest brother Sam was born while we lived in the Black Hills. Iris and her friends had gotten hold of a Ouija board and used to play around with it, asking if certain boys at school liked them, which teachers they would get in the next school year, and things like that. My mom was expecting at the time, and so Iris and her friends inquired about the baby's gender and name. The Ouija board said that the baby would be a boy and my parents would name him Sam. When they got the information, we all ran to my mom to see if they were going to name the baby Sam if it was a boy. My mom said no, they were thinking of Shannon for a girl, and they didn't have a name picked out yet for a boy. A few months later, Sam was born. When we asked my mom about Sam's name, she said she didn't even remember us asking her about it and she wouldn't name a baby something based on a Ouija-board prediction. She said that she and my dad had chosen the name because Sam's birthday was close to the feast day for St. Samuel, a Catholic martyr.

The only other weird thing from Sam's toddler years is that my mom got him a Bozo the Clown doll that none of us liked. I don't know exactly why, but it seemed menacing—its face was too animated or something. Sam threw the doll in the closet and said he hated it. No one played with the doll for thirty years—it was in with all the other toys in my mom and dad's toy closet, but all of the grandkids in our family, starting with Molly and Jack, had the same negative response to the clown doll that Sam did. Molly called it the devil doll. When I was helping my mom go through some closets at her house a few years ago, we decided to get rid of Bozo. We were going to give the doll to Goodwill, but after thinking about it, we decided to just throw it away—which is never done in my environmentally thrifty, reduce-reuse-recyle family. My mom and I just didn't think some other kid should be saddled with such a creepy thing.

In 1971, my dad found a good job back in Minnesota. Although we were sad about leaving the Black Hills and our friends, we knew we'd be returning to both new adventures and familiar faces. So we packed up again and returned to St. Paul, the heart of family gatherings and Irish parties.

*My brother Sam (right) and cousin Sigrid (left)
at the pasture gate, Lake Elmo, Minnesota, circa 1975.*

The goblins of her fancy lurked in every shadow
about her, reaching out their cold, fleshless
hands to grasp the terrified small girl
who had called them into being.
Lucy Maud Montgomery, "Anne of Green Gables"

❧

Bloody Mary and Ouija Boards:
Stories from the Doomed Farmhouse

Back in Minnesota, we moved into another old farmhouse outside the small town of Lake Elmo. Hidden away at the end of
a long dirt road, surrounded by fields and woods, the farmhouse on the
hill was the perfect place to live, as far as I was concerned. It had an
apple orchard, pear and plum trees, wild grapes, a strawberry patch, and
a big flower garden. There was a ramshackle barn, a pump house, pot-
ting shed, corncrib, and assorted other outbuildings that made perfect
forts and hangouts for kids our age. Everywhere you looked, there was a
place to explore or disappear to or claim.

My brothers and sisters and I made friends with the kids from the
neighborhood at the foot of the hill. They were happy to be able to
explore the cool territory that had been off-limits to them when the
Millers, an older couple, lived there. To add to the drama and fun of our
secluded home, the quarter mile-long dirt driveway cut through some
woods, where a drainage tunnel ran under the road. The big metal tunnel was about four feet high, almost tall enough to stand up in. We kids
had meetings in the tunnel and used it to spy on people coming up the
hill and as home base for games like tag and ditch. But the tunnel, and
all the terrible possibilities it held, was so scary to walk past at night that

after dark, my girlfriends from the neighborhood and I always escorted each other home. We'd generally walk together as far as the tunnel, then we'd turn and run for our homes from there.

There was a pond in the neighborhood with a beautiful stone farmhouse next to it. Farther down the service lane was an abandoned house that was about a five-minute bike ride away. A hobo was camped out in the empty house one summer, and we all made the pilgrimage to check out the situation. My girlfriends Sue, Deana, and Chellie and I got scared as soon as we saw the sleeping bag and empty booze bottles in one of the rooms. We heard that some of the older kids from the neighborhood had actually seen the vagrant who was staying there, and he had yelled at them to get out. At the eastern edge of our neighborhood was a Catholic church that most of the local families attended, including ours. The church had a cemetery that we occasionally walked through on our way home from church. I feel it is more than happenstance that for most of my life, I've lived within a block or two of a graveyard or funeral home. I think exploring the relationship between the physical and spirit worlds is one of my life's themes.

We knew from the time we moved into our Lake Elmo farmhouse that eventually it would be torn down to make way for a golf course and a bunch of fancy houses. How long we got to stay in the house depended on when the market was right for Mr. Stedwright, the millionaire who owned the farm, to sell the land to a developer. Mr. Stedwright also owned the sand plant that my dad managed, and occasionally he'd drive out to the plant in his baby blue Cadillac and shoot the breeze with my dad and the men who worked there, as well as any truck drivers who happened to be around. Sometimes, when I was climbing the trees in our apple orchard or swinging from the rope swing in our hayloft with my friends, I couldn't bear the thought of such a cool place being torn down and turned into a golf course. Living in a doomed house gave even ordinary experiences a bittersweet intensity.

There was a tall old elm in the field right beside our house. The elm was dead but had remained standing. Vines had started to grow on it, and it was a favorite perch for hawks and crows and other birds. To me, the old elm symbolized strength and stoicism, a ghost tree that refused to give up, even though by some measure, it was already gone. It seemed a fitting sentry for our living-on-borrowed-time house. When I had a hard time at school or with my friends, or a really good time, or something interesting or weird happened, I found myself telling the elm tree about it as I walked past. If my day was ordinary, I just said hello as I walked by. Now, nearly four decades later, our Lake Elmo farmhouse is still the house that, along with my grandma and grandpa Haraldson's house, most often haunts my dreams. (More on Grandma and Grandpa Haraldson's house in the Leprechauns and Sugar Cookies and Ghost Girl chapters; also see photo gallery.) In his book *Ecoshamanism*, James Endredy makes the excellent suggestion that people create a cognitive picture map of an outdoor place they connected with in the past as a powerful way of re-establishing a bond with the energy and spirit of that time and place. I want to create a map of our old farm and the neighborhood as a way of expressing gratitude for the gifts and lessons of living there, and of sharing some of the stories from our childhood with my young nieces and nephews.

It was while living in this old farmhouse that I started actively trying to communicate with the spirit world. We moved there the summer before I went into fourth grade. For a while, my sisters Betsy, Maggie, and I used to play with the Ouija board almost every day. It was mostly Betsy and me playing since were older, with Maggie usually relegated to the role of observer. We must have gotten our hands on the Ouija board that Iris had used in the Black Hills. We were convinced of its ability to see into the future after it predicted our brother Sam, and consulting the Ouija board became a part of our after-school routine. Even though most of the information was difficult or impossible to prove (like being told we would be rich when we grew up or what our future husbands' initials would be), we found the Ouija board to be very chatty and friendly. It got to the point where the Ouija board seemed to have an actual identity and personality, and it would start our sessions off with comments like "You girls look nice today." This unsolicited form of communication should have been a warning, but we didn't catch on.

Not long after the Ouija board took on this more independent, familiar tone, Betsy and I started to wonder who the Ouija board communicator really was. Was it the ghost of a person? A spirit who only existed because of the game? One afternoon we decided to ask.

"Who are you, Ouija board?" Betsy and I sat cross-legged on the floor of our bedroom with our hands on the planchette. Our younger sister Maggie sat beside us. We were excited to find out more about the spirit who talked to us every day. We had absolutely no idea of the shock we were about to receive. The planchette started to move.

"L. U." We read the letters out loud as the planchette slowly made its way across the board and stopped at each one.

"C." Betsy and I looked at each other. Lucy? That was an old-fashioned name. Maybe it was the spirit of a little girl. But the planchette moved again.

"I." That was weird. Lucy with an "i"? That wasn't very old-fashioned. Maybe we were getting a last name? The planchette slowly pushed forward.

"F. E. . . ."

Lucifer! I don't remember if Betsy or I screamed it first. The Ouija board and planchette clattered to the floor. Betsy and I were on our feet in a second, running out of the room as fast as we could. Maggie ran behind us, yelling, "What happened? What just happened? Who was it?"

After we got outside and collected ourselves a bit, we told Maggie that Lucifer was another name for the devil. We knew we had to get rid of the Ouija board. We decided the best thing to do was to get it out of the house, throw it straight in the garbage, and pray that it never came back. It was very hard to go back to our room and get the Ouija board, but we did it. I almost expected the Ouija board to be gone, but it was lying on the floor of our room where it had fallen, seemingly inert. We threw it in the silo of our barn and never told our mom what had happened.

As scary as it was to have the name Lucifer come through the Ouija board, neither my sisters nor I became possessed by the Ouija board spirit, haunted by evil entities, or experienced any other ill effects. So it didn't stop us from trying to communicate with the spirit world in other ways. My friends and I held séances in the closet and tried to summon Bloody Mary through the bathroom or bedroom mirror. The séance closet was in the room that Maggie and Betsy and I shared. It ran under the eaves and was completely dark and cramped and filled with piles and piles of stuff, from Barbie doll cases to boxes of books and papers to suitcases. We always lit a candle (which as an adult makes me cringe, given the many flammable objects in the closet) and tried to summon spirits of people we knew who had died, or sometimes of famous people.

One time, my friend Deana (see photo gallery) and I were conducting a séance. After we had asked a spirit to give us a sign that it was there, I saw green hands coming from behind Deana and wrapping themselves around her neck. Before I could scream, she screamed. We jumped up and ran out of the closet and into the bathroom (one of the few places where you could have privacy in our house). We were scared but excited and laughing from nervousness.

"Did you see the green hands?" I asked Deana. Deana said she hadn't seen anything, but she had felt something starting to choke her, and that's why she screamed.

Deana was also with me the first time I saw the energy grid, an element of the astral world that looks a moving chicken-wire fence made of light. I've seen the energy grid hundreds of times throughout my life and have come to believe it's some sort of underlying structure for the astral realm or possibly an information system for things that exist on the astral realm. I have seen it in the periphery of my vision, especially if I'm tired or stressed out. I've seen it both underlying and running through the geometric light shows that I sometimes see at night or early in the morning, with either colorful twinks and squiggles of light or actual objects or forms, such as an Egyptian ankh or the infinity symbol. (These geometric lights are described at length in my first book.)

And I have found these astral light shows to sometimes be responsive to my thoughts. Once, when a geometric light form was morphing into different shapes, I thought, "Wait! It's going too fast. I won't be able to remember this." And the light form repeated the action, but this time in slow motion. I've now reached a point where I can see the forms while I'm awake and describe what I'm seeing while I watch it.

But a moving chicken-wire fence made out of light was the last thing I expected to see in the girl's bathroom at my old grade school. Deana and I and a couple of other friends snuck into the girl's bathroom during recess one day to summon Bloody Mary. We must have been sixth graders—I don't think we would have been brave enough to commandeer the bathroom, even for just a few minutes, if we weren't. The Bloody Mary séance was really popular at the time. It involved standing in the dark in front of a mirror and chanting, "I don't believe in Bloody Mary. I don't believe in Bloody Mary." This taunt was designed to entice Bloody Mary, the former Queen of England, to come back from the dead and appear in the mirror. My friends and I never really talked about what might happen after she appeared, like whether or not Bloody Mary could get out of the mirror and chase after people.

The excitement level was high as we shut the door and turned off the light. Actually, just being in the school bathroom in the dark was so unusual that it set the stage for weirdness. We started our chant. After only a minute or two, someone screamed, and we hightailed it out of the bathroom. I don't remember anyone saying afterward that they saw Bloody Mary. What I saw was the energy grid, which struck me as a weird, but not scary, thing to see. As we ran out of the bathroom, I could still see the grid of light moving in front of and around me. It made it hard to run. It felt sort of like being at the roller-skating rink when they projected moving lights onto the floor, which always tripped me up.

I view the Bloody Mary experience as opening a door for me as far as developing astral vision. I think one of the aspects of the experience that made it more powerful than other séances I'd done was that I was with a group of girls instead of just one friend. The few times in my life when I have participated in it, I've found group chanting to be a really effective technique for raising energy. I also think the collective energy of my friends and I was heightened to begin with, since none of us really ever broke any rules at school, and we knew we'd probably get in trouble if we were caught summoning the ghost of a murderous monarch in the girl's bathroom.

. . . . . .

One of my first precognitive visions happened at school as we were discussing plans for our spring concert with our much-loved choir teacher, Miss Jacobson. The theme was popular American music through the decades. Deana and I already had a duet together, "In My Merry Oldsmobile," with two boys from our class acting as the old-fashioned suitors. My mom and Deana's mom, Cookie, got together and made matching long dresses for us. Two of our friends, Judy and Billy, were chosen to dance to "The Band Played On," the song my great-grandma Maggie had loved to sing. As soon as Miss Jacobson assigned the dancing roles to Judy and Billy, I saw an image in my mind of the two of them waltzing on a spotlit stage, Billy in a dark suit and Judy, who had strawberry blond hair, in a long lavender satin dress. On the night of our concert, as I watched Judy and Billy waltzing across the stage, I realized I was seeing the very same scene that I had seen in my mind months earlier. It had the same visual elements, from the lighting to the dress, right down to the same perspective, with Judy and Billy being on the left side of the stage.

This experience made me trust my perceptions of two other visions I'd had earlier while living at Lake Elmo. The first was seeing an old house that I knew wasn't there. I had gone to play in the fields behind our house, which I had done many times before. As I came up over a hill, I saw a house that had never been there before. It was a white, two-story house with peeling paint and broken windows. It looked abandoned. I ran back to my house to call Deana to come see it, but when we went back together, it was gone.

Another weird experience was a "time-slip," which two of my sisters have also experienced. (Their stories are told in the "Laughing Boy and Girl in the Glass" chapter.) I had been playing at Deana's house. Deana's family was colorful and fun, and they had an interesting house, filled with taxidermic animals and birds and fish in nearly every room but the kitchen. They also had funny pictures and sayings on the walls. In the bathroom, a wall hanging said, "The Gundersons don't swim in your toilet, so please don't pee in our pool," and a bumper sticker in one of the bedrooms said "FOXY" and had a picture of a sexy red fox on it. Deana's dad, Len, looked like a movie star and drove a '68 Chevy Impala convertible. Deana's mom, Cookie, loved to sing and had a strong soprano voice and a bunch of old 45 rpm records—Bobby Vinton, Tammy Wynette, Sam the Sham and the Pharaohs—that Deana and I would sing and make up dance routines to. In addition to a sewing machine, which all of the moms in the neighborhood had, Cookie had a knitting machine. The Gundersons also had an electric organ in their living room that Cookie would play quite often. Once, I got to go with Deana and her family to Chippewa Falls, Wisconsin, where both her mom and dad had grown up. Deana and I got new summer scarves for the trip, but the wild, windy ride in the back of the convertible ripped my scarf right off my head. Even so, flying down the road in Len and Cookie's convertible with the top down was way cooler and more fun than trucking around town in my family's big yellow station wagon with faux wood-grain panels.

When I left Deana's super air-conditioned house one day after she and I were done playing, I was temporarily blinded by the hot, bright sunshine. (Deana's family kept their house really dark, with all the shades pulled down, when the air conditioner was running.) I kept blinking, trying to get my eyes to adjust to the sunlight. When I could see again, I realized something was off—our neighborhood looked different somehow. I was still walking down Deana's driveway when I realized what was different—the trees were smaller and younger, and even the landscaping at my friend Sue's house next door was different. I knew it was still our neighborhood, but it seemed like I was seeing it as it might have looked ten or twenty years earlier. The houses didn't seem exactly right either, but I couldn't pin down what the difference was. I was just starting to get rattled by the implications of this when I got to the end of Deana's driveway and stepped onto the main road. Suddenly, everything was right again. I looked back at Deana's and over at Sue's house. Now they looked exactly like they were supposed to look. I ran until I got a few houses away, then turned around again. Everything was still normal. Now that I was feeling a little more secure, I thought about how interesting the experience had been. I thought about going back to Deana's driveway to see if things still looked weird from that vantage point, but I was too scared. In this instance, I don't think I traveled backwards in time. I think I just tuned in to a scene of our neighborhood from the past.

Another unusual thing that happened when I was living at Lake Elmo was the spinning bed sensation. The phenomenon would commence as soon as I got into bed. I knew my bed wasn't actually spinning, but only because I would open my eyes to check, since it felt so real and so intense. I wonder now if the spinning sensation was a form of astral projection. I have a theory that I may not have been in my body very much as a teenager. I came up with this idea for two reasons. First, because of what psychics have told me about most of my spirit energy being outside my body. Second, because out of all my brothers and sisters, Betsy and I are the ones who had (and still have) the most astral visions and out-of-body experiences, or OBEs. We were also the only two kids in our family who did not have major skin problems as teenagers. My theory is that hormones didn't affect us as much when we were teens because no physical issues affected us as much—we weren't as connected to our bodies as most people are.

We did have a house full of teenagers at Lake Elmo, at least four or five of us at one point, and there was a lot of intense energy floating around for a while when we lived there. Sometimes, lying in bed at night, I felt like there was a dark thing moving through the house, always coming up from the first floor, stealthily making its way through the rooms as it searched for someone to land on. I said a protection prayer for everyone in the house when I felt this predatory presence, and if I felt like the prayer didn't take, I said it again. Although I didn't know any magical theory at that age, this is a basic protection technique. While I didn't really think it was a ghost flying around our house, I thought it was more like anger or churned-up emotions that could still do harm at some level. And even though the experience felt somewhat threatening, I believe going through it honed my ability to sense and work with energy.

We moved out of the Lake Elmo farmhouse in 1977 and into a big house out in the country in Wisconsin. My parents still live there. Our Lake Elmo farm was razed sometime in the late eighties or early nineties, and a golf course and high-end condos were built on the property. Our farmhouse wasn't torn down for the golf course, but it was moved to an empty lot in a nearby neighborhood. I've never gone to look at it. The woods are still there, but the tunnel is gone, and what used to be our dirt driveway is a paved road. A Best Buy store and shopping mall was built right next to the church, and a huge three-story assisted living complex towers over the beautiful old stone farmhouse that served as the cornerstone of the neighborhood.

I still see my friends Deana, Chellie, and Sue. Deana had a ghost experience at my house in Sibley sometime in the first few years after my family moved in. After I realized my house was haunted, Deana was really reluctant to spend the night. She would come over for visits but leave before dark. After my kids and I had lived here for a few years, I finally convinced her to sleep over one evening. We hadn't had any ghostly activity for a while, and I figured things would stay quiet. Deana is very outgoing and bubbly and funny. Along with her very warm, positive vibe, she has a fabulous figure, which may be one of the reasons why something invisible groped her in the shower, an experience no one else has had at my house.

Ironically, Deana had become so afraid the night before the shower incident that she decided to sleep downstairs on the couch alone instead of up in the guest room. Despite her fear, the night was uneventful and she slept well. But while I was making coffee the next morning, Deana came running out of the bathroom in a towel, wild-eyed and with shampoo still in her hair. "I thought you said the ghost was gone!"

"Ummm—isn't it?" I said.

"No!" Deana's voice was kind of screechy. "I had my hands up, putting shampoo in my hair, and something grabbed me from behind! I turned around and there was no one there. That's when I grabbed the towel and ran out of the bathroom." Luckily, Deana has taken the incident in stride and added it to the repertoire of weird and outrageous experiences that she's had in her life. Deana has never been bothered again by spirits at my house, although she has never showered here since that day, either.

Deana's mom, Cookie, died in September of 1998. Christmas had always been Cookie's favorite time of year, and sometime around Christmas of 1999, her spirit paid Deana a visit. Deana was at home in the kitchen, thinking about her mom and how much she missed her. Suddenly, Deana heard the grandfather clock in the living room chiming. She knew the clock had been broken for months, so she walked over to see if her husband, Ben, had fixed it. The clock was still chiming, but the chimes, which were the parts in need of repair, were still unattached and lying inside the clock. Deana felt that this unusual event was a message from Cookie, and she told her mom how much she loved and missed her. When her husband got home, Deana told him what had happened. Ben looked at the clock and said it would be impossible for it to make any noise at all. So Cookie, being a good mom, helped Deana out—she came back while Ben was home and rang the chimes again. This time, Deana was on the phone with Cookie's sister Maxie, and Ben was in the kitchen. When the grandfather clock started chiming again, Deana said Ben ran into the living room to see how it was making the noise. After seeing and hearing it for himself, he agreed that there was no possible way for the clock to be chiming, and he was willing to believe that Cookie's spirit might have stopped by to say hello.

One night in 2003, I woke up and saw a carousel made of colored lights suspended in the air in my room. It was stunning and whimsical, and I recorded the experience in my datebook, where I write down dreams, messages, and any weird experiences. Then I forgot about it.

A few years later, Deana asked me if I could help her get in touch with her dad's spirit. Unfortunately, although I have experienced a lot of spirit communication in my life, my skills aren't developed enough to be able to see and talk to spirits whenever I want to. The communication happens when the spirits come to me—so far, anyway. Deana was a little bummed. She asked me if I had gotten any messages from her dad. She gave me the date that her dad passed away, and when I looked back in my old datebook, I saw the note about seeing the carousel made of colored lights the night after he died. Along with a description of the carousel, I had written a note that said I thought of Len Gunderson (Deana's dad) while I was looking at it, and the carousel lights flashed.

I don't remember why I didn't tell Deana about this when I learned that Len had passed away. His health had been failing for a while, and his last few years were pretty rough. Deana was his primary caretaker, and she was pretty exhausted herself at the time. They had a private service for the immediate family only. Maybe I was going to wait until things had settled down to tell her. I felt bad that I had forgotten to tell Deana about this experience, but then it occurred to me that maybe she heard the story at just the time she needed to hear it. Deana was very excited when I told her about the vision. She told me that her dad always got her a carousel for her collection. We agreed that the beautiful carousel was a sign that her dad was happy and doing fine.

After my book *House of Spirits and Whispers* came out, my publisher, Llewellyn, ran a spooky story contest in which people submitted their true ghost stories to me. All the stories were published on Llewellyn's website, and the top five or six stories won Llewellyn books as prizes. One of my favorite stories in the contest was written by a woman whose Great-Aunt Lydia had appeared in her room the night she died, "all dressed up in an old-style dress with a little pillbox hat, purse, and matching gloves." I loved it that Aunt Lydia brought her purse to heaven! I've told all my friends I plan to do the same.

Shortly before Len Gunderson died, one of Deana's aunts dreamt about him. In her dream, Len was in bed and not doing well, and Cookie was in the room with him, wearing a red dress. Deana told her aunt that red was her mom's favorite color. Len passed away a few days later, and ever since I heard the story of this dream, I've liked to imagine that Cookie was waiting for him on the other side, looking sharp in a pretty red dress, in the passenger seat of a foxy '68 Impala convertible.

Dinner party at Grandma Dorrie's house, circa 1948.
Left to right: Great-Aunt Norah, her daughter Penny, Big
Uncle Thomas (standing), and unidentified dinner guest.

They may forget what you said, but they will
never forget how you made them feel.
Carl W. Buechner

❧❦❧

Leprechauns and Sugar Cookies:
Grandma Dorrie's House

My grandma Haraldson—Grandma Dorrie—was one of my favorite people in the whole world, and I still consider her a role model and an inspiration. She was a loving and generous-spirited person who loved to throw parties and have fun, and talked to all of us grandkids about interesting things like dreams and ghosts and fairies and leprechauns. She told us what the world was like when she was a child and shared her opinions on current world events. From her, we learned that, although there are hardships in life, the world is filled with magic and fun if you just know where to look. Grandma Dorrie told us that whenever you spent the night in a new bed, you were granted a wish that would come true. And that you could make a bird "freeze" like a statue if you threw a pinch of salt on its tail. At family dinner parties when we helped Grandma Dorrie fill the candy cups with mints and nuts, she always said, "Let's have a little taste" instead of "Wait until you've finished your supper."

Grandma Dorrie made popcorn balls at Halloween and a special red and green version at Christmas. She always had homemade cookies on hand—sugar cookies with colored frosting, gingerbread boys and girls with licorice mouths and buttons made of Red Hots candies, and my favorite, chocolate krinkles, which were like tiny crinkly brownies with powdered sugar on top. Grandma Dorrie was genuinely interested in our stories and questions, was positive and encouraging, and always told us we could do anything we set our minds on doing (see photo gallery).

Grandma Dorrie and Grandpa Anton Haraldson's house was like a movie-star home, and one of the games my sister Betsy and I loved to play when we stayed there was to pretend we were movie stars. Two of the five bedrooms had ornate dressing tables with big mirrors, flowered wallpaper, and taffeta bedspreads, and we pretended those were our dressing rooms. Grandma and Grandpa Haraldson's house also had a sparkling chandelier in the formal dining room, high ceilings, beautiful cut-glass windows that made rainbow prisms, and a piano room. There were ceramic leprechauns hidden in the plants, and small bisque dolls with ribboned hats and colorful ball gowns in a box in the playroom closet that Grandma let us play with even though they were breakable. When Betsy and I went there for visits, we ate fancy ham salad sandwiches and drank pop with our meal. We got to eat lunch in the living room with a TV tray so Grandma could watch her program, *Days of Our Lives*. (Even though she generally remarked on how dumb soap operas were at least once during the show.)

Grandpa Haraldson would tell us true stories about growing up in a northern Wisconsin town where the Chicago gangsters had a summer cabin, and how he had a job one summer driving one of the Mafia guys around. He made up stories with interesting characters, such as a mobster named Four-Fingered Louie. Grandpa Haraldson was an attorney, and sometime during the 1950s, he and Grandma invited one of his clients, a rather eccentric old woman, to be their houseguest. Mrs. Baits was a skinny and rather severe-looking woman who dressed in black and spoke French a lot of the time (see photo gallery). Her stay was going to be just for a day or two while my grandpa got her affairs in order, but Mrs. Baits liked it at my grandparents' house, and soon her brief visit had turned into weeks, then months, then years. My mom's younger siblings, who were still living at home at the time, were none too happy about the situation, as one of Mrs. Baits's idiosyncrasies was her insistence on using a chamber pot at night and dumping its contents out the second-story bedroom window in the morning. She would also come downstairs when my teenage aunts and uncles had friends over, and sit on a chair with a stern expression on her face. Mrs. Baits had a fascination with the Dionne quintuplets and had an impressive collection of pictures and articles about the five identical sisters. She finally moved out when her health failed.

Grandma Dorrie had two precognitive experiences that I know of. The first involved my aunt Veronica, who is also my godmother, and took place in the mid-1950s. Veronica had decided to become a nun. Veronica told me that when she made the difficult decision to enter the convent, she wasn't looking forward to telling my grandparents. The order she chose was very strict, and Veronica felt that my grandparents would not understand her decision. She came home from college with the idea that she would break the news to them that weekend. But when she started telling Grandma Dorrie about it, my grandma already knew. She told Veronica she had a dream that Veronica became a nun and she was hoping it wasn't a premonition. Veronica did enter the convent, but after spending some time in the program, she decided that it wasn't her true vocation, and left.

Grandma Dorrie's other experience was a dream visit from a young woman's spirit—the seventeen-year-old sister-in-law of my uncle Jerry. Jerry is my mom's youngest brother and had been married to his wife Diana for about five years at the time. We had all met Diana's sister Jillian at the groom's dinner and wedding. Jillian was my age, so she and I had hung out together. She was really pretty and confident and happy, and over the next five years, at family parties, Diana would let me know what was new in Jillian's life. Sadly, Jillian died in a car accident when she was seventeen. Even those of us who didn't know her well were shocked and saddened by the news because she was so young and such a great person. Grandma Dorrie took the news especially hard—maybe because she had dealt with so much tragedy and loss in her childhood—and said she was so upset that she couldn't collect herself and just kept crying. Grandma Dorrie had a dream that night that Jillian came up to her and comforted her, telling her she was all right and not to grieve for her. In the dream, Jillian had short hair, when in real life, she'd had long hair. My grandma did feel better after this dream, and when she told Diana about it, Diana told my grandma that it really must have been a visit from Jillian, because Jillian had gotten her hair cut not long before she died.

I believe that one of Grandma Dorrie's gifts was to serve as a source of comfort and strength to the dying, for her family, and for others whom she loved. Her childhood experiences with death before she was thirteen years old revealed her incredible courage and sensitivity in end-of-life matters. She was in the room with her siblings James and Ethel when they died, because after *her* childhood experience, Great-Grandma Maggie just couldn't be in the room with a dying person. We don't know if Grandma Dorrie was in the room with her aunt Annie when she died, but as far back as people can remember, she was always at the hospital when a family member passed away. I believe Grandma Dorrie's role as a source of strength for the dying has continued after her own death, as sort of a psychopomp, or guide of souls. On at least a couple of occasions, she has appeared in dreams before a family member dies. I had a dream (discussed in the upcoming Snowy Owl chapter) in which she gave me a message though a friend that "something important" was going to happen in a week. And my uncle Jerry had a vivid dream a short time before my cousin Alexandra passed away that he met Grandma Dorrie's spirit walking down a hallway with her arms around a woman. He couldn't see who the woman was, but Jerry said it was clear to him that Grandma Dorrie had come to help someone cross over to the other side.

My grandparents' house had a few unexplained ghostly things happen there. Besides me seeing a little ghost girl run past the bathroom (discussed in the Ghost Girl chapter), my Grandpa Haraldson, who lived in the house for a number of years after my grandma died, said he heard voices occasionally. I was really curious to find out who the voices might be or what they were saying, but Grandpa Haraldson said he couldn't understand them.

One of the freakiest experiences that happened at Grandma and Grandpa Haraldson's house happened to my mom's youngest sister, Kathy. I knew there was a story about the record player starting up by itself and playing a crazy song, but I couldn't remember the details. Kathy filled me in on the details with the following email:

> When I was young and alone (at Grandma and Grandpa's house), Anton's stereo began to play by itself. Heidi, my dog, started barking like crazy, with hackles up, at the dining room wall with the chimney. The song was "Lovely Hula Hands," and the thing that was really weird was that it was on one of those old hi-fis, the kind where the 33 record had to manually be put on a spindle, up high, and then the arm had to be swung over to drop the record, and of course none of this was done. The on button wasn't even turned on.

When Aunt Kathy's sons Stuart and Eli were young and shared a bedroom, they saw a ghost one foggy morning. Kathy and her family lived out in the country, and one morning when Stuart and Eli first woke up, they saw a figure in the fog, out under the pine trees in their yard. Their bedroom was on the upper level of a split-level home, so the boys were looking down at whatever it was. The figure seemed to be picking up pinecones. Both boys saw this thing, and both were super scared at the time. In the past, two old homes had existed on the farm property. One was a cabin that was more than a hundred years old (which my aunt Kathy and her husband, Tom, had sold to someone who carefully took it down and reassembled it elsewhere) and the other old farmhouse they had torn down to build their home. My cousin Stuart now speculates that maybe there was once a garden in the yard where they saw the man, and what they saw was somehow related to a scene from the past of a man picking vegetables or fruit from a garden.

My cousin Clint, whose dad is my mom's brother Anton, is a strong, tall auto mechanic with a shaved head and a biting sense of humor. He's about the last person you'd expect to have ghost problems, but his house has ghosts the way my house has ghosts. Clint bought his early 1900s-era home back when he and my youngest brother, Sam, were both single. Sam rented a room from him. One night, shortly after they moved in, Sam was away on business. Clint woke up in the middle of the night because he heard someone walking around in the hallway out-side of his room or possibly in one of the other upstairs bedrooms. Clint said he somehow knew it was a guy, maybe because of the heaviness of the steps, and that it sounded as if the man was dragging a heavy chain on the floor. The chain-dragging noise was all the more weird because the hallway was carpeted. Clint knew he was home alone, and he was freaked out. He said he rolled himself up tight in his covers, making himself into a "Clint burrito." He believes that this first ghost visit was from the original owner.

The next thing that happened, not long after that, also happened when Sam was gone. Clint said Sam was gone again and might have been out on one of his "multiple attempts at finding a wife." Clint was watching TV and drinking beer, and he got up to use the bathroom. Since he was home alone, he didn't bother to close the door, but the bathroom door closed itself while he was in the room. Clint didn't think too much of it at the time, attributing the door closing to drafts. But a few hours later, the same thing happened again, and he got spooked. He went through the house to make sure no one was in there with him and checked the windows and doors. They were all closed. Clint attributed this ghostly door-closing behavior to a female spirit, and I agree with him. When you're dealing with spirits, you have to make educated guesses about who they might be (or who they were) based on their actions and other factors, such as where they're hanging out.

Clint believes his next ghostly encounter was also a female ghost. This time, Sam was home, but in bed in his room on the second floor. Clint was in the basement, drinking beer and watching the big-screen

TV. He had fallen asleep on the couch when he was awakened by a gentle touch on his shoulder or leg (he can't remember which). He said the experience felt friendly, like the spirit was trying to help him wake up so he could go to bed and get a few hours of quality sleep before having to get up for work in the morning.

When my brother Sam met Jenny, they got married and bought a house together, so Clint was now alone in his haunted house. During that time, Clint said there was a period of about a week where every night when he got home from work and opened the back door, it sounded like there was a party going on inside. Just like my childhood experience in South Dakota, he could hear people talking and laughing, glasses clanking, the usual party noises. The noises continued as he made his way through the kitchen and dining room. When he got to the foyer, the house instantly became silent. I asked Clint if he felt left out that the party ended as soon as he arrived. He said he interpreted it as recognition from the ghosts that he had worked hard all day and needed his rest.

After Clint's wife Nina moved in with him, she got a ghostly welcome. The first night she was there, Nina woke up because she thought she felt someone stroking her hair. When she realized Clint was sound asleep, she thought she must have imagined the experience. The next night, the same thing happened, but this time, as she lay awake trying to figure out why she could feel someone stroking her hair, she heard a man's voice say hello. Clint said Nina's screams woke him up, and she spent the rest of the night stuck to him "like a wood tick." He told Nina, "Well, the ghost knows you're here," and that she should let it know what was and was not acceptable. Nina informed the ghost that she didn't want to be touched, and she has not been touched since. Clint said they still have lots of paranormal activity in their house, but it comes and goes. They have a lot of the traditional ghosty stuff, like lights flickering, doors slamming by themselves, and pounding in the walls. Recently, both Clint and Nina have also seen a spirit. Clint was in the living room one night and got the feeling he was being watched. He looked up, and out of the corner of his eye saw a man in a gray or brown suit standing in the foyer. Another time, Nina was home alone, and she saw the same man going up the stairs. She became very upset when she realized that the spirit she was seeing had a head wound and was bleeding profusely. Clint said they made some inquiries and discovered that one of the sons of the previous owner had died in Vietnam when he was struck by debris from a land mine. Clint told me things have been quiet around their house for a while but telling the stories would probably get things riled up again.

My great-aunt Norah's children have had some precognitive or mystical experiences, too. In 1978, right after Christmas, my mom and I were talking, and my mom asked me if I was expecting. I said, "No! Why do you ask?" She said that at Christmas, Norah's oldest daughter, Penny, had told a few people that I was expecting another baby. Molly was about eleven months old at the time. It turns out that Penny was right. I was already pregnant with Jack; I just didn't know it at the time. When Norah's husband, Victor, passed away, Norah and his kids were in the room with him. Their daughter Bev said her mom was leading them in saying the rosary, and when her father died, Bev saw a golden light fill the room. And when I was consulting psychic Patrick Mathews about some family questions, including a question from Norah's youngest daughter, Kay, about her daughter Kylie, he said Kylie's Grandma Marie had come through with some advice. I asked him if he was sure about the name, since I was expecting to hear Norah or one of the other Irish relatives' names. He checked and said no, it's Marie. I said, I wonder if that's Norah's middle name, even though it didn't sound right. Patrick said good-naturedly, "Don't argue with a ghost! Let's just see what she has to say." When I told this story to Kay, as soon as I said the name Marie, she gasped.

"Is that your mom's middle name?" I asked. Kay told me it wasn't Norah's middle name—it was the name of Kylie's grandma on her dad's side.

My mom's cousin Margie had a supernatural experience when her father died, even though he and her mom, Nellie, had been divorced for many years, and Margie hadn't seen him very often in the previous decade. In the mid-1970s, when Margie was married to her first husband, Stan, she woke up one night at 3 AM and said, "Someone close to me is dead!" Margie said she hadn't dreamt of the death and didn't know who it was (except it was someone really close—even closer than a cousin or friend). She was absolutely certain someone had died, and she was afraid it was her mom. But she didn't want to call her mom, because of the late hour and because if her mom was okay, then her mom would start worrying about who it might be, and if she wasn't okay, Margie didn't want to know because she couldn't handle it. The next morning, Nellie called Margie and told her that her father, who had lived in South Dakota for many years, had died the previous night. He had lived at a veteran's home, and they told Nellie that he had been out for a walk at 3 AM when he apparently had a stroke and died.

Nellie had also tuned in to Margie needing help one night. It happened when Margie and Stan were dating. One of Stan's friends had a Shelby Mustang, and they were out with him, riding around on a crooked road. He took a corner too fast and hit the guardrail. Margie said the guardrail probably saved their lives, as the car was so smashed up it wasn't drivable, even without going over the steep embankment. Margie called Nellie to tell her what had happened. Nellie said she already knew Margie had been in an accident. She had felt it and was worried sick, waiting for the call.

It is my belief that we still have a relationship with our family and friends in spirit. We can honor and connect with them by telling their stories, and we can help them by saying prayers and remembering them with love. In return, I believe our family in spirit wants to connect with and help us, too. Grandma Dorrie's spirit has come through for both my mom and me when we needed her. Twice, my mom has heard Grandma Dorrie offer specific advice in response to health issues my mom was having, and the advice turned out to be correct. And one evening when I was feeling completely stressed out about the book release party I was getting ready to host at my house, a clear visual image of my grandma Dorrie appeared in front of me. I was in my kitchen, but I saw my grandma clearly in my mind. She was smiling and said, "Annie, relax! Your party is going to be great. And I'll be here helping." It was the first and only time I got a spirit message like that from my grandma Dorrie, and it was a huge help to me. In the final week before the party, whenever I felt overwhelmed, I reminded myself that my grandma was helping me, and she had always thrown fabulous parties. And my book release party, which more than three hundred people attended, went off without a hitch.

Grandma Dorrie died in 1989, just a week or so after she hosted a formal Christmas Day dinner for the usual crowd of sixty or seventy people. Maggie was staying with Molly, Jack, and me at the time, and I came home one night to find them all sitting at the kitchen table, somber and quiet, with a single candle lit. I asked Maggie was what was going on.

"Grandma died," Maggie said.

I didn't know what Maggie was talking about at first, because Grandma Morgan was already in spirit, and I knew she couldn't mean Grandma Dorrie. I said something like what do you mean, and Maggie said, "Grandma Haraldson died. She and Grandpa were on their way out to dinner, and she had a heart attack." I walked out of the kitchen and went into my bedroom and cried. I couldn't imagine the world without Grandma Dorrie in it. I couldn't even imagine what our family would be like without her. It seemed like Grandma somehow made everything okay with her strength and love. And one of my biggest dreams was to get published and dedicate my first book to Grandma Dorrie. But I hadn't yet made that dream come true, and she was gone. I cried some more, then went out to the kitchen to sit with Maggie and my kids.

After Grandpa Haraldson died some years later, a bunch of Grandma Dorrie's belongings were given to me, partly because I have a big, old-fashioned house that has extra room and an attic, and partly because of how close I was to my grandma. I love looking around my house and seeing Grandma Dorrie's formal sofa and beautiful Irish rose lamps. Vintage knickknacks that she gave me long ago, including my favorites, a cat in a seashell and a baby riding a swan, are on display in the china cabinet in my dining room. Her fur coats and silk and taffeta dresses, including the one she wore to the first formal dance she attended with my grandpa in the 1920s, are in the guest room closet.

When my mom and aunts were cleaning out my grandparents' house after my grandpa died, my sister Betsy and I went down to take pictures before the house was put up for sale. It was really heart-wrenching to think of Grandma and Grandpa's house being gone forever. As we made our way through the house, down in the basement, tucked back on a shelf in a storage room with a bunch of gardening stuff, we found the pink planter in which Grandma Dorrie had always planted clover. We picked up the planter to take it upstairs with us and discovered a little ceramic leprechaun half buried in the dirt. I brought him to my house, washed him off, and once again, he is bringing good luck to the plants in my parlor and to anyone who happens to discover him in his leafy hideaway.

I did eventually write a book, and my grandma was one of the people I dedicated it to, in this way: *This book is dedicated to my grandma Dorrie, the most loving, interesting, and fun grandma a girl could have.*

Years ago, psychic Patrick Mathews told me that my grandma Dorrie and I have such a strong bond that she is like a guardian spirit for me. Every now and then, when I walk through the doorway between the kitchen and the parlor or when I'm upstairs by the linen closet, I get a whiff of my grandma's Emeraude perfume, and I know that Grandma Dorrie is paying a visit, her love and support still present in my life.

My mom (right) and her sister Veronica in front of
their first home in southern Minnesota, circa 1940.

Magic lives in curves, not angles.
Mason Coole
❧

The Ghost Girl and Other
Spirits Out of Time

Can a person be haunted the same way a house can be haunted? Why do some spirits spiral through time, coming back again and again? One of the best ghost stories in our family is the story of the little ghost girl that followed my mom around for decades. My mom remembers first seeing the little girl in the 1970s or '80s at the house in Wisconsin where she and my dad have lived for more than thirty years. The little ghost girl appeared to be five or six years old. She was dressed in old-fashioned clothing and had long brown braids. Even for a spirit, the little ghost girl was unusual. For one thing, whenever my mom saw the ghost girl, she seemed to be tagging along and even participating in whatever my mom was doing. The other odd thing was that my mom never saw the ghost girl's face—she didn't have one. It wasn't like there had been any trauma to her face, but where the ghost girl's face should have been, there was nothing.

In the late 1990s, when my niece Gwendolyn was eight years old, my mom was driving her back home after a visit. After making sure Gwendolyn was securely seat-belted in the back seat, my mom got behind the wheel. As she did, she saw the little ghost girl, visible only from the waist down, climbing into the front passenger seat beside her, apparently settling in for the three-hour ride to Stevens Point, Wisconsin. The little girl was wearing old-fashioned wool leggings, which was appropriate, given the season. I asked my mom if she said anything to the ghost girl. My mom said she hadn't said anything because she didn't want Gwendolyn to get scared.

My brother Randall also saw the ghost girl. Randall lives in California, but he saw the ghost girl when he and his girlfriend at the time came back to Wisconsin for a visit. In my parents' house, you come in the front door and then go up a flight of steps to get to the main living level of the house. It's not an open staircase, and when my brother got to the top of the steps, he stuck his head around the corner and called out hello. Down at the far end of the house, my brother saw a little girl with long brown braids scurry into my mom and dad's bedroom. Randall heard my mom yell hello from a different bedroom, just as his girlfriend reached the top of the steps behind him. My mom came out to welcome Randall and his girlfriend, but when Randall asked who else was there visiting, my mom had no idea who he was talking about. Randall said he had seen a little girl in a white nightgown run into my parent's room, but my mom insisted she was home alone. They went down and looked through the three bedrooms and two bathrooms at that end of the house, but they didn't find the little girl. At the time, Randall didn't believe in ghosts, and we gave him lots of razzing about seeing one. Afterwards, I asked him if he still believed there was no such thing as a ghost, and he said, "You see one little apparition and people expect you to change your entire worldview!"

Randall's experience made me reconsider a weird incident from my childhood. When I was six or seven, my sister Betsy and I were staying at Grandma and Grandpa Haraldson's house for an overnight visit, which we loved to do. It was the home my mom had lived in from the time she was seven or eight until she left for college. Betsy and my grandma and grandpa and I had stayed up late to watch *The Tonight Show* on my grandparents' color TV. We were eating vanilla ice cream with Hershey's chocolate syrup on top, all of which was complete decadence and total fun. I finished my ice cream first, brought my dish to the kitchen, and went upstairs to get ready for bed. I was standing in my grandparents' fancy bathroom, feeling like a movie star as I brushed my teeth in front of the dressing table mirror. Out of the corner of my eye, I saw a girl in a white nightgown run past the open bathroom door. I jumped, even though I knew it had to be Betsy. I couldn't believe she had snuck past me somehow and gotten into her pajamas so quickly. I yelled Betsy's name, but when she didn't answer, I got scared. I yelled her name again as I ran out of the bathroom and down the stairs. When I made it into the living room, I saw Betsy sitting in the same spot she had been before, still in her regular clothes and still eating ice cream with my grandparents. As soon as I realized it wasn't Betsy who had run past the door, my stomach dropped. I didn't go upstairs alone at night at my grandparents' house for a long time after that. Randall's reference to the little girl in a white nightgown scurrying down a hallway sounded so much like my experience that it made me wonder if this also might have been an early sighting of the ghost girl.

Eight years ago, I read a book on a versatile and simple energy healing practice called Reiki, and I called my mom to tell her about it. I also wanted to see if my mom would be interested in taking a Reiki class with me. We both laughed when my mom told me she had never heard of Reiki until a week or so earlier, but she had just read a book on it and was going to ask *me* if I wanted to take a class on it! We viewed the serendipitous timing as a good omen and signed up for a class. We soon completed our level 1 Reiki training, which explored Reiki principles and history and taught how to use basic Reiki techniques for healing people, animals, and plants. A year later, my mom and I completed level II Reiki training, which covered higher-level healing practices, such as doing distance healing and using Reiki on the energy systems of the human body, such as the aura and chakras.

The night after my mom and I completed our level II Reiki training, my mom was sitting in the rocking chair in her bedroom. One of the

Reiki symbols our teachers had passed to us was one that allows insight into the past and the future. This symbol also is a key to access the Akashic Records, an astral record of everything that's ever happened in the entire universe—sort of like a library of the collective unconscious. My mom decided to use to this powerful symbol to try to connect with the ghost girl and see what her story was.

As my mom rocked in the chair, she drew the symbol in the air with her hand. She said she felt the little girl's presence immediately, although at first she couldn't see her. A few seconds later, the girl materialized, and for the first time, my mom saw the ghost girl's face. It took my mom a second to realize what she was seeing, but when she did, she was shocked.

The little ghost girl was my mom. She was my mom at age five. The ghost girl looked really sad and lost. My mom was completely shaken up, but she held her arms out to the girl, and the ghost girl climbed into my mom's lap. Then she disappeared.

My mom told us this story while we were all at my sister Betsy's house. It was summer, and we were out on the dock. My mom's story was so engrossing that none of us noticed my brother Dan slip in the lake. He swam silently under the dock where we were standing, reached up through the dock slats, and poked at the bottom of my niece Gwendolyn's feet with cold, wet fingers. Gwendolyn let out a bloodcurdling scream, and so did the rest of us. It was very therapeutic, and after we got done screaming, we all laughed.

So how did my mom become haunted by herself? I believe the little ghost girl was part of my mom's own soul. There is a theory in shamanism that a portion of our soul's energy can break off due to trauma or grief and remain stuck in a certain time or place. Soul retrieval is a shamanic ritual to call back and restore lost soul parts. When my mom was five, her parents moved from the Irish family homestead in St. Paul to a small town sixty miles away in southern Minnesota so my grandpa could start his own law practice. My mom spoke of how difficult it was for her to adjust from living in a bustling household of Irish relatives who doted on her and her sister Veronica to living in a relatively empty house in a quiet town. Rocking and swinging are two of the techniques shamans can use to enter into a trance state. I think, without even knowing such a thing existed, my mom did her own soul retrieval from the rocking chair in her bedroom. She has not seen the ghost girl since the night the girl disappeared in her arms.

. . . . . .

I have been told by two psychics that the spirit of a young girl is in my house, although I've never seen her. In May of 2006, my friend Dave Schrader from the "Darkness on the Edge of Town" radio show came to my house with two psychics and a film crew. The psychics were C. J. Sellers, who has since appeared on the hit A&E television show *Paranormal State*, and Robert Baca, a well-respected psychic from Iowa. Neither was told where they were going, and neither had read my book. As soon as Dave asked Robert to be a part of this project, Robert started psychically picking up information about my house. He immediately described my house to Dave, who then called me and asked if the description was correct. It was. At the time, I was being exceedingly careful about maintaining my privacy, so I was a little freaked out. Robert Baca also tuned in to a strong male spirit in the back kitchen—Leon, the main ghost at my house. Robert also convinced me of his skills when he told me there was a mentally ill male ghost who had lived in my house in the 1860s or '70s. He said the ghost was telling him about a bad spirit in the house without realizing he was referring to himself. In other words, the spirit had a split personality. I thought of Dark Man and the entity that had pinned me down in my bed. But at the time Robert told me this, I thought my house had been built in the 1880s. So I just listened with the idea I'd do some digging later to see if I found any information that resonated with Robert's impressions. The following year, I found out from the town historian that my house was actually built in the 1860s, and one of the original owners, a military man, was mentally ill, at least at the end of his life. He had died in what was then called the Minnesota Asylum for the Insane in St. Peter.

When Robert and C. J. came through the house separately, each saw a little girl spirit. Robert tuned in to her right away. He said she was around four years old, and she considered me sort of a mom but not exactly. He said I was taking care of her. He asked me if I had ever lost a baby, and I said I hadn't. He said, "Do you know if your mom lost a baby soon after you were born?" I said I didn't think so, since my next younger sister, Betsy, is an Irish twin, meaning we were born less than a year apart. (She's eleven and a half months younger than me, and as kids we thought it was cool to be the same age for two weeks every year.)

Robert said the spirit girl's name was Sarah and I had agreed at some level to take care of her. He also stated, correctly, that Sarah told him I referred to my cats as my kids and called out, "Hi kids, I'm home!" when I came home from work. The idea of a little ghost girl in my house was intriguing, although I was a little disappointed I hadn't picked up anything about her myself. I thought about my mom and her ghost girl experience, and wondered if I had a ghost girl of my own. I did have a vivid dream when I was in my early twenties that we were all at a big party at Great-Aunt Norah's house and my mom came walking over, leading a young girl by the hand. The girl had dark eyes and strawberry blond hair and was wearing a pale yellow chiffon party dress. My mom asked me if I would be willing to take care of the little girl. I could see that the girl was strong-willed and even obstinate, but I felt I could handle her, so I said yes. I kept a close eye on the little girl for the remainder of the party, watching her to get a better idea of her ways so I could figure out how to best care for her. When it was time to go, she didn't want to leave. I picked her up and told her to say goodbye to my mom. She stuck her chin out and didn't say anything. I knew the moment could easily turn into a contest of wills. I said, "Say goodbye, Annie." As soon as I said my own name, I realized I was holding a younger version of myself.

At the time I had this dream, I had never heard of soul loss or soul retrievals, and it just seemed like an interesting dream. I've always made endless fun of the concept of an inner child. I tell people I have an inner

Norwegian farmer instead. But I paid attention to the dream message anyway, which at the time I interpreted as encouragement to use my experience and life wisdom to direct my willpower, rather than the other way around. Robert's impression of a young spirit following me around that I was taking care of made me wonder if I'd been wrong. But with cameras rolling and two separate ghost tours of my house to complete before the night was over, I didn't think it was the ideal time to bring up the ghost girl possibility.

After Robert had completed his walk-through, someone drove him back to his hotel and picked up C. J. When C. J. came through, she mentioned that there was a little girl spirit following me around, and that I was taking care of her. Dave Schrader and I looked at each other.

"Do you get a name?" Dave asked.

"I don't usually get names," C. J. answered. "Oh, wait! It's Sarah. She just told me." Three years later, I still have not seen or felt Sarah. But I do believe that Robert and C. J. both tuned in to a spirit child named Sarah, and that if there's a reason for me to see her, I will.

Years ago, I was told by a psychic who does readings with a regular deck of playing cards that part of my life's purpose was to care for children, both on the physical and astral realm. Another possibility that occurred to me regarding Sarah is that she is connected to a friendly spirit, Petros, whom I've seen twice. When well-known ghostbuster Echo Bodine was at my house, she told me that Petros and I had shared a life in Peru, and his soul was a friend of my soul (a transcendent concept that resonates with me). Echo said Petros had tried to make his presence known to me many times, and that he had not incarnated with me in this lifetime because he was taking care of a young girl in the spirit realm. Maybe Sarah is that girl.

. . . . . .

Another ghost mystery that involves spirits seemingly lost in time is the appearance of the old-fashioned spirit sisters in my house. The Hartnett sisters lived in my house in the late 1800s and early 1900s. One of the sisters wrote her name on an antique seed poster on a door that was hanging upside down in the basement dirt room. (The cover of my first book is a photograph of the antique seed poster. If you look closely, you can see Julia Harnett's initials on the seed poster girl's forehead and "lia" from her name written on the seed poster girl's chest. See photo gallery.) The night we brought the door upstairs was the first time I saw the spirit sisters. They appear as young women with long dresses and pompadour hairdos. I've seen one of the sisters on three separate occasions and another sister once. The old-fashioned spirit sisters are always floating in the air, always transparent, and always completely white. When I did research for my first book, I found a picture of one of the sisters in a class graduation portrait from 1907 (see photo gallery). All the girls in the picture are wearing long white dresses and have pompadour hairdos. Between the clothing and hairstyle match, and the timing of the first sighting, I felt we had correctly figured out the identity of the old-fashioned spirit sisters. But when I did more research on the Hartnett family, I discovered that two of the three sisters had lived to be old women, and if I had moved to town fifteen years earlier, I might have run into them at the grocery store! It messed up my romantic notion of young spirit girls lost in time.

So why did I see the spirit sisters as young women in turn of the century dresses and hairdos rather than as grandmothers in 1970s wear? I don't think I'm seeing simply lost soul parts, because the spirit sisters project a strong sense of self-possession and self-confidence. They're animated and interactive and whole. I think they occasionally like to return to their former home for a visit, and when they do, they materialize in a way that reflects how they looked when they lived here. Their nineteenth-century clothing and hairstyle was also a form of communication. It helped me figure out whose spirits I was seeing, which I appreciate.

Linda Drake, a down-to earth psychic from Austin, Texas, told me when she visited my home that it holds a powerful attraction for the people who once lived here, and that many of the former homeowners and tenants come back just because they loved it so much. When I hosted an open house event for Sibley's sesquicentennial a few years back, a very nice family told me that their aunt Gertrude had lived here in the 1950s. They showed me a picture of Gertrude and asked me if I had seen her spirit around, since she had loved the house so much. I told them I hadn't seen any spirits that looked like her but that maybe her energy was still part of our house, as I had named my fabulous, room-encircling philodendron Gertrude, and I had never named a plant before.

"Well, she loved plants, so that would be perfect!" her niece told me. When I mentioned that I had since bought another philodendron and named it Matilda, Gertrude's niece gasped. "That was her daughter's name! And Matilda was here all the time, helping her mother."

Encountering ghosts is like being in a three-dimensional puzzle; four-dimensional if you count time as a dimension, which is usually a relevant factor with ghosts. Ever since we brought the antique seed poster door up from the dirt room, it's been on display in the parlor. I put a spotlight on the door, and when I entertain, I turn on the light so people can see Julia Hartnett's faded signature scrawled across the seed poster, written in loopy cursive letters. The spirit sisters communicate by turning the spotlight off and on, and we have learned through experience that they are most responsive to women and children. I feel like the parlor is the right place for the antique seed poster door. A parlor is old-fashioned to begin with, and mine has a distinctly feminine vibe, with muted pink walls, a piano in the corner, African violets in the east window, and lots of green plants all around. It seems fitting that when the spirit sisters come back through time for a visit, they make their entrance through a wonderful old homemade door in the front parlor.

*Molly and neighborhood friends having pillowcase races
in the back yard, Hudson, Wisconsin, circa 1984.*

> The more enlightened our houses are,
> the more their walls ooze ghosts.
> *Italo Calvino*

❧

The Haunted Trailer
and Other Weirdness
in Wisconsin

Roberts

When I got married to John, Molly and Jack's dad, we lived in an apartment in St. Paul for six months, then bought a trailer in the small town of Roberts, Wisconsin. The trailer court was on the edge of town and, even though I knew it wasn't exactly fabulous to live in a trailer, I liked our sunny and cheerful little home, which was all done up in '70s décor. All the appliances plus the toilets, sinks, and our fancy garden tub (which had two steps leading to it) were harvest gold. The walls were brown paneling, and the color of basically everything else—carpets, linoleum, curtains, wallpaper—was burnt orange. Jack and Molly were both babies when we lived there, and orange is still their favorite color, which must be some sort of testament to the positive vibe of our trailer house (see photo gallery). Although I never experienced any paranormal activity in our place, it was rumored that there was a haunted trailer in our park—on our street but down one block. I heard about it at one of my neighbor Dani's Tupperware parties. Dani was a colorful person, a Tupperware lady with long, dark hair and gypsy looks. She had loud fights with her husband and swore in regular conversation. Dani had a beautiful, junglelike flower garden on her lot that was the envy of the trailer park. Her Tupperware parties were well-attended and sort of wild, with alcoholic beverages and lots of laughter and occasional loud arguments. At the time, I wasn't old enough to drink, and we didn't have extra money for Tupperware products, but I was so intimidated by Dani that I didn't know how to refuse her invitations. I did enjoy listening to Dani's stories, which is how I learned about the haunted trailer.

Dani had actually been inside the haunted trailer (none of the rest of us had). She said that the bedroom was haunted, and the wife realized it first because her jewelry box, which was the kind that played music, started acting up. The first thing the jewelry box did was to start playing by itself. Eventually, it escalated to "jumping around" on top of the dresser. The husband, who didn't believe in ghosts, finally saw it, too. I did hear that the couple was having problems and eventually split up, but I heard nothing more after that.

I used to think about the haunted trailer when I went to pick up my mail. The mailboxes for the entire park were on a central street, only three or four lots away from the haunted trailer. I was glad I didn't live right next door to the haunted trailer, and in my mind, I sort of "blurred out" our trailer so if the ghost tuned in to me because I was thinking about it, it wouldn't follow me home. I think it was instinctive to do this rudimentary shielding technique.

John and the kids and I only lived in our trailer for a year before we purchased a house in Hudson, Wisconsin, through a first-time home-buyers program. When our marriage ended after nine years, there were times when I wondered if I had misperceived our relationship the entire time. I started to question my judgment. During one of these periods of doubt, I had a strange dream in which I found myself back in our trailer in Roberts. I was standing in the kitchen, but everything was dark. I opened the curtains and saw that someone had put a piece of cardboard over the window. I took the cardboard off and was able to see clearly. As

I turned around, I noticed food and plates on the table, as though someone had gotten up in the midst of a meal. All of a sudden, I thought, "What am I doing here? I don't live here anymore." Then I heard the front door opening. I stepped back into the hallway so I wouldn't be seen, and as I did, I realized there was a woman with her back to me, standing at the sink doing dishes. Then I saw my former husband John come in through the front door and pick up baby Molly. When I realized I was seeing an everyday scene of my family from the past, I glanced over to the woman at the sink. She turned around, and I saw that she was me. The dream version of me went up to John, and they hugged. The best part of this dream was that I could actually feel the love John and I felt for each other and remember the emotional bond that we had shared. It made me realize that the decisions I had made regarding matters of love and trust were good ones, even though our marriage didn't last. The dream ended with the dream me catching sight of the observant me. I didn't say anything to the dream me, because I didn't know what would happen—I didn't want to scare myself. But the dream me just smiled and said, "May I help you?" I remembered how trusting and accommodating I had been, and it made me a little sad. When I woke up, I searched my mind for anything that had happened when we lived in the trailer that might have been the flip side of my dream—in other words, me perceiving a visit from my future self, or even a presence in the trailer watching me—but I never have come up with anything. Still, because it was so emotionally powerful, I feel this healing experience was a more than an ordinary dream.

My Parents' House

My mom and dad live in the country, on the outskirts of a small town on the western border of Wisconsin. They have had so many haunting experiences at their house, it's hard to know where to begin. They bought their house in 1977. It was kind of a sad situation for the seller. She was a woman whose husband had died. He had been a newly remarried widower when he built the big country house for himself, his two teenage sons, and his new wife. Unfortunately, the man died before the house was completely finished. I don't know if his widow didn't want to be out there alone after the last two kids moved out or if there were estate matters to settle, but the man's dream of a country house for his family ended with his death. That's when my parents bought the house. I believe that the man who built it is the male spirit that my parents encounter most often.

When we moved into the house, seven of us kids were still at home, and the big rambler with five bedrooms and three bathrooms felt like a fabulous luxury. It was a seventies-era house through and through, with a sunken living room, psychedelic flower wallpaper in the downstairs hallway, a red, white, and blue bedroom, and orange and black carpeting in the open living room and dining area. My parents have been redoing the interior over the years, and one of the first things to go was the Halloween-colored carpeting. My folks' house seems to be getting more haunted as time goes by, but maybe it's just that the ghost couldn't make itself heard over the noise of five teenagers plus two boys aged eleven and six.

My mom has had more paranormal experiences in the house than my dad, but my dad has had a few weird experiences as well. More than once, he has had to take a look around to make sure the loud crashing noises he and my mom heard were caused by a ghost and not an intruder. Probably the most common haunting behavior at my mom and dad's house is hearing heavy footsteps coming up the stairs, then walking down the hallway to their room. My mom has actually felt someone sit down on the bed, which seems intrusive, but it's relatively common spirit behavior. (Twice, I've awakened at my house to find a spirit sitting at the foot of my bed. One time, it was my great-grandma Maggie, who I was surprised but happy to see. The other time, it was an incredibly sad woman from the 1940s who, despite her sorrow, seemed more like an image or imprint than anything else. Both experiences are covered at length in my first book.) My mom's impression is that the spirit that has sat on their bed is male.

My mom and I send emails back and forth when weird stuff happens. It's a quick way to share our stories; plus, for me, it's helpful to have a written record of events. Here's a typical email that I got from my mom in December 2008:

> Also have been a lot of hallway, stairs, and other walking noises, and drawers opening and closing. Last night, I was reading in the sunken living room and I heard steps coming up the stairs, going back to the bedroom, and just assumed that it was O. T.* getting ready to shower because of noises of drawers opening and closing, ditto closet doors. I thought nothing of it until about 5 min. later when he came upstairs from the garage. No message from whomever was banging the drawers!
>
> Love, Mom

Elsewhere in this book, I tell about my mom seeing the spirit of her dog George and hearing a man clearing his throat on the same night my niece Gwendolyn heard the same sound at my house. Some of the other unusual ghost activity my mom has experienced includes seeing the bathroom shower curtain, which was pulled closed, ripple all the way across its length, as though a breeze had blown behind it. This happened in the middle of the night, and the bathroom window was closed at the time. My mom did not open the curtain to see what was behind it.

On at least two occasions at my parents' house, a picture has flown off the wall, not in front of my parents but when they're in the next room. When they have come out to investigate the crashing noise, they've found a picture lying on the floor in the middle of the room. My mom believes in paying attention to possible messages, so she always calls whoever is in the picture, just to check in.

---

* My dad. His nickname is Old Timer, or O. T. for short.

One of the more unusual things that happened at my mom and dad's house was the night the guitar strummed itself. My mom was home alone at the time. There was an acoustic guitar at my folks' house, left there by either Molly or my brother Randall. My mom woke up and felt like someone was in the room with her. She went into the hyperalert state that you go into when you feel threatened and looked around. (My mom leaves a lamp on at night if she's home alone.) She didn't see anyone, but she heard one strum of the guitar, as if someone had brushed a hand across the strings. Her dog George was at the foot of the bed, so she knew it wasn't him, and he doesn't usually play the guitar anyway. Nothing more happened that night, but my mom had a hard time getting back to sleep.

One of my favorite ghost stories from my parents' house was the night my mom grabbed a ghost. She woke up and saw a man's hand reaching out for her. At first she thought it was my dad's hand, which still would have been weird, but then she saw that the hand had no arm attached to it—it was just floating in the air. And—here's one of the things I love about my mom—she grabbed the hand as hard as she could. She said it felt like a regular human hand, with skin and muscles and bones. It wasn't freezing cold or anything ghostly, but it did disappear in her hand. When my mom told me about this, I laughed because it was like the opposite of a ghost story—the living person freaked out the ghost, instead of the other way around.

On a similar note, I recently had a vivid dream in which I woke up because I heard voices coming from my bedroom closet. It sounded like two men having a conversation. When I knocked on the closet door and asked who was in there, they stopped talking.

"What's that?" one of the voices said to the other.

"A ghost!" the other voice said, then laughed.

"Leon?" I said. "Is that you?"

One of the voices answered, "How about Ted Steinmeyer?" Ted and his wife, Gertrude, were the owners of my house in the 1950s, before Leon Kuchenmeister and his wife bought it in 1963. I opened the door, and Ted and another man came out into my room. They both seemed like decent fellows, if a little perplexed by the situation. Ted asked me if I was a ghost.

"Sort of," I replied. "I bought your house in 1994. And I've been living here for fourteen years."

Was I a ghost? My house is energetically unusual. If spirits from the past can come through time for visits, maybe my astral body can go backwards in time to visit past homeowners as well. The possibility had never occurred to me before I had this dream.

Hudson

The first real house that John and I owned, which we bought after living in our trailer, was a small 1950s bungalow in Hudson, Wisconsin. Its most charming feature was a double fireplace. One side of the fireplace faced the dining nook, and the other side, the living room. I was happy to have a house, but we had a lot of work to do. The people who'd lived there before us kept thirteen dogs in the house (ten puppies and three adult dogs), and the basement and garage were filled from floor to ceiling with the family's stuff. They had even used the yard as a storage area, keeping three old Jeeps behind the garage, along with a professional-grade freezer. After we moved in, we cleaned, painted, replaced all of the flooring and window treatments, cut down a dead tree in the yard and planted a new one, and slowly made the house cheerful and inviting. The best change we made, besides planting several trees in the yard, was adding a wildflower garden that encompassed the entire south side of the house. It was shaped like a half circle, with a smaller circle of flowers in the center, all outlined with sandstone that I got from the sand plant where my dad and John worked. It was designed to have blooming flowers all summer long, and it was spectacular.

Molly was not quite two and Jack was three months old when we moved into the house. Molly was already starting to display some of her intuitive abilities. The very first demonstration was in our car in the parking lot of the grocery store. I had both kids with me, and Jack, who was a baby, had gotten fussy in the store. I shopped as quickly as I could, but I was pretty stressed out by the time we got through the checkout line. As I was putting Jack in his car seat, I caught a glimpse of my reflection in the rearview mirror, and my eyes looked wild. It caught me off-guard because I thought I had been doing a good job managing a stressful situation. Since I'm a writer, I started thinking of the moment as though I was writing about it: "She caught a glimpse of herself in the rearview mirror, and her eyes revealed her true feelings," and so on, reworking the sentence in my mind a few times. Molly, who was already in her car seat sucking her thumb, pulled her thumb out of her mouth and said, "Mom, I want to see your eyes" in a very conversational way, as though she had read my mind.

I said, "What?"

Molly said again, "I want to see your eyes!" It was a little nerve-wracking to think of having a child who could read my mind. But my sister Betsy has had the same experience, with her daughter Christine responding verbally to her thoughts.

The second thing Molly did that demonstrated her psychic abilities was when she tried to make a record not skip with her mind—and succeeded. She was three or four, and the kids had a record that they loved. We played it over and over, and eventually, it got scratched. There was one place on one of the songs where the needle got stuck, and I'd have to come and move it or the music would just keep repeating. One day, I was in my room putting on makeup and came out to the living room because the record was getting to the skip point. Molly was standing facing the stereo with her eyes shut tight. I asked her what she was doing.

She said, "I'm trying to make the record so it doesn't skip." I was completely taken aback, because I couldn't imagine what had even given her the idea. I asked her how, and she said, "With my mind." I asked her where she learned that, and she said she didn't know. It was then that I realized the record had gone beyond the skip point—and had not skipped. If I had a young child now, I would work with her or him in a low-key and supportive way to develop this kind of skill. But at the time, I didn't know how to respond to what had just happened. I didn't discourage Molly, but I didn't follow up on this demonstration of psychic ability in any structured way, either.

One day, Molly told me that someone named Wendy had come into her room the night before. I assumed Wendy was an imaginary friend until Molly told me that Wendy had hurt her.

"What?" I asked, a bad feeling coming over me.

"Wendy hurt me," Molly repeated.

I asked Molly how Wendy had hurt her.

"She stuck sharp things in my head, " Molly said. "She told me it would be okay." When I asked Molly to show me where, she pointed to her temples. I checked them and was relieved to see no sign of trauma. Molly said first Wendy rubbed her temples, then she stuck something sharp in them. I asked Molly what Wendy looked like.

"I don't know," Molly said. "I've couldn't see her face."

Again, I had a sinking feeling. "Why not?"

"She wore a cloak," Molly answered. "It covered her face."

I told Molly that friends don't hurt their friends, and they don't keep their faces hidden. I also told Molly that if Wendy ever came back, she was to let me know immediately, and together, we would make sure that Wendy never hurt her again. Maybe Wendy got the message, because Molly never saw or sensed her again.

So, who or what was Wendy? We never have figured it out for sure. One possibility that has occurred to me is that Wendy was drawing energy from Molly. That is one of the primary threats that astral beings pose to those of us in physical bodies. One night last summer, I had a very frightening experience at my house. I woke up really scared without knowing why. Then I saw a small hooded being beside my bed and got the distinct impression it was trying to pull my astral body out of my physical body. In my sleep, I had curled up tight in an instinctive effort to protect myself. I started praying and asking for protection. Suddenly, the hooded being was "removed" from the room. This is the only word that I can think of to describe what happened. It looked like the hooded entity was lifted away by some force that I couldn't see or feel, like someone picked it up and took it out through the ceiling. As I watched it flying backwards and upwards out of my room, I saw that there were three or four other hooded beings behind it. They disappeared in the same way.

Nearly every psychic who has come to my house in Sibley tells me there are at least two or three portals here (portals are openings between the physical and spirit worlds). When psychic Linda Drake visited my house, Leon, the main house spirit and my ally in the spirit world, told her, "This house is filled with doorways. It's like Grand Central Station for ghosts." I realized after the encounter with the small hooded creatures that I needed to do some prayer and protection work around my house and property. (At the end of this book are techniques for blessing and protecting one's home.)

Another weird instance at our house in Hudson was when Molly's cousin Jill spent the night. The girls were around eight and nine years old when this happened. The night seemed pretty normal from my busy-mom perspective. After supper, the girls spent a lot of time in Molly's room, with lots of giggling and chatting going on. Once, they ran out of the room screaming and laughing, but I didn't pay any attention to it because it seemed like sleepover fun and games. What I didn't know was that the girls had been in Molly's bedroom, just talking, when they saw a playful procession of little people, about six to eight inches tall, come out of the closet, hop down off the dresser, and march in a line around the room. The little people were in "old-fashioned clothes" and they were all barefoot. Molly and Jill both saw them (and Jill, as far as we knew, was not psychic and didn't even believe in that kind of stuff). The little people seemed unaware of Molly and Jill. One of the girls threw a piece of popcorn at the little people, which had no discernable effect on them but caused Molly and Jill to run screaming out of the room in anticipation of what the little people might do. The girls didn't tell me about what they saw because they didn't want me to make them go away. When the girls went back in Molly's room, the little barefoot beings were gone. Molly and Jill tried to get them to come back, and even looked for them in the closet, to no avail. Eventually, the girls went to bed. They did not experience anything else strange that night.

So why would two young girls see tiny barefoot people marching around a room? I have to admit, at that point in my life I might have thought the girls were pulling my leg with their story. I did not think that our house in Hudson was haunted—and yet, we sometimes heard small knocks and noises coming from the closet where Molly and Jill had seen the little people emerge. The closet had a nearly impossible-to-utilize design. Built in a space above the basement steps, it could only be accessed from a door in Molly's room that was about three and a half feet off the ground. The closet was deep but had almost no floor space because on one side, there were three built-in shelves, and on the other, the steep slant of the basement steps. Basically, you either had to stand on a chair and shove stuff in the deep closet as best you could or climb into the closet, standing at an angle or perched on the narrow framework. I generally chose the former option, so the closet was sort of a jumbled hodge-podge of holiday decorations and things we didn't need very often. I always attributed the noise to piles of stuff shifting and falling. But it's interesting that the noisy closet was the point of origin for the little barefoot people. Their appearance didn't coincide with any significant anniversaries (that we know of) or presage any dramatic events. Molly says now that if she had to guess, she'd say the little people represented some sort of fairy energy. That makes sense to me. I believe everything that exists in the physical and spirit world is essentially some form of energy. Just as a spirit may appear in many different forms (in human form or as a ball of light, to name just a few possibilities), I think house spirits, or brownie energy, may appear as little people. (More on this possibility a little later in this chapter, when I talk about Theosophist beliefs.)

Not long after Molly and Jill saw the little people, we had another weird experience that started in Molly's room involving an old-fashioned paper Christmas angel. The Christmas angel had been in the funky closet with the other seasonal stuff, but one year we decided to hang it on Molly's wall instead of putting it away with the other holiday decorations. It wasn't until the morning after the angel incident that we put the whole story together. I had gone to bed quite late (I was taking weekend college classes and working at the time, so I usually did my homework after the kids went to bed). I woke up in the middle of the night to the sound of something flying around my room. I ducked under the covers and listened, trying to figure out what I could be hearing. I finally concluded that either a bat or a bird had gotten into the house. My bedroom door was shut, and I figured whatever it was would probably stay in my room. I decided I would deal with the situation in the light of day and resigned myself to sleeping completely under my covers, so whatever was swooping through my room couldn't actually touch me.

The next morning, when I woke up, it took me a minute to remember the night's events. I took a quick look around my room, then ran out, shutting the door behind me. On my way out, I noticed the paper angel from Molly's room lying on my floor. The kids were watching TV. I told them not to open the door to my room because I thought either a bat or a bird was trapped inside. I told Molly that her angel decoration was on the floor of my room and I would get it after I dealt with whatever was in my room.

Molly said, "I don't want the angel decoration in my room anymore. I slid it under your door last night." When I asked her why, Molly told me the angel had moved by itself the previous night, swaying from left to right while still hanging on the wall. Molly did the logical kid thing, asking the angel, "Are you really moving?" The angel nodded her head yes. Molly asked the paper angel one more question (she no longer remembers what it was), and the angel shook her head no. That's when Molly, who has always been very brave, ripped the angel off the wall and slid it under my door. At some point in the night, knowing nothing of what Molly had experienced, I woke up and heard the sound of something flying around my room. I didn't turn on my light because I didn't want something flying into my hair when I made my way across the room to the light switch.

Did Molly and I tune in to some astral being or energy that was communicating through the paper angel? The angel's actions—swaying back and forth, answering questions, and flying around—don't really make any sense, unless something just wanted to get our attention. I had always loved that paper angel because of the Christmas memories she held and her quaint, old-fashioned charm. But after searching my room and finding neither a bat nor a bird, I was freaked out enough that I threw the paper angel away.

. . . . . .

Not everything that we initially thought was weird or scary turned out to be. Molly and Jack's dad, John, is colorful character, a funny guy, and a great storyteller with a wild streak to boot. One night, I was talking to our friend and neighbor Sonya, an elementary school teacher with a garage sale-ing soul, when I heard someone pick up the other phone. I asked Sonja if she heard it, and she said, "Yes. Does someone want to use the phone at your house?" I told her the kids were in bed and I could see John from where I was standing, so I knew he hadn't picked up the other phone. I asked Sonya if she had another line at her house, and she said she did in the basement. She said, "Hang on, I'm going to put the barricade in place." (The barricade was a two-by-four with a piece of carpeting stapled to either end that Sonya's dad had made. When Sonya put it between her basement and kitchen doors, no one could get in.) Sonja had no more than said these words when her line went dead.

"Quick, run to Sonja's and make sure she's okay!" I yelled at John, filling him in on the details as he ran for his shotgun. He had been on his way to bed, so he was in his long johns, but he threw on his winter boots and raced out the door. He jumped in his truck and drove to Sonja's (four houses down) in his underwear to confront whoever was in her basement. Sonja was waiting for him at the side door. She had gotten freaked out when her line went dead, but she did get the barricade in place. She took it down so John could come in. He told Sonya to be ready to call the police as he headed into the basement. Sonja was just starting to remind him that her phone was dead so she couldn't call the police when John slipped (because his boots had snow on them) and slid down the basement steps on his butt, his gun on his shoulder. Luckily, no one was hurt. Sonja found out later that her line went dead because the phone cord was old and needed to be replaced. That's why we heard the strange noise, too.

· · · · · ·

Two of the weird paranormal experiences I had while living in Hudson were related to the escalating troubles between John and me. The first was a bad dream that I had that seemed to bleed into Jack's consciousness. Jack was about five years old at the time. My dream started with John and I having an argument. As the argument escalated, he and I were transformed into pure energy, floating blobs of light that were mostly red but pulsed or throbbed with other colors too. The angrier we became, the darker and more intense the red color got. Finally, John, in his pure energy form, left the house. I floated around, still angry. Then I saw Molly and Jack on the couch watching TV, and I floated over to them and settled on the couch next to Jack. Even in my dream, I felt like it was dangerous to expose my kids to that kind of negativity. My dream ended when Jack woke up in real life, yelling, "It's coming to get me, it's coming to get me!" Once awake, I felt really bad. Jack could not describe what had been coming to get him in his dream, but because of the timing and the fact that Jack had never before woken up with a nightmare, I felt he had been affected by my bad dream. I had not heard of auras at that point in my life, but I believe my dream illustrated what was going on energetically between John and me, and the effect it was having on Molly and Jack.

I also think it was the stress in our house that caused Molly's picture to act out. We had a close-up photograph of Molly's face with her warrior princess expression that we'd had blown-up to a 11 x 14 size. We put it in a Plexiglas freestanding picture frame, along with a big photograph of Jack in the same type and size frame. Molly's picture was constantly falling down from the mantel. Sometimes I'd find it lying facedown right below the mantel on the hearth, and sometimes it would be out in the middle of the floor face-up. After this happened a few times, I started to wonder if something was going on. I swapped out Molly and Jack's pictures to see if the mantel was just off-kilter on one side. But it wasn't—or, at least, Jack's picture stayed put, while Molly's started falling off the other side of the mantel. After John and I separated, our house felt much more peaceful. And Molly's picture stayed put.

One of the most dramatic experiences I had while living in Hudson had many elements for which I had no explanation at the time. It happened one night when John and I were in bed. He was asleep, and I had just set my book down and was dozing off. Suddenly, my body went on high alert, like I sensed imminent danger. I strained to listen or see something, but I didn't see anything out of the ordinary. Suddenly, the walls of our bedroom seemed to melt away, and I could see our back yard. In real life, it was summer, but the outdoor scene I was seeing was winter. As I struggled to figure out what was going on, I saw a man standing in our yard in the shadows and knew immediately that he posed a threat. He was wearing old-fashioned clothing and carrying a long gun. I knew that the man was John, but I also knew John was beside me in bed. I was going to wake John up when the man outside lifted his gun and shot me in the back. This is where the weirdest part of this very bizarre experience comes in. I was experiencing the scene from more than one perspective simultaneously. I could see the man in the yard, I could see John and myself lying in bed (from above), and I could see inside my body, where the bullet had nicked my spine and lodged in muscle. I also knew logically that I couldn't have been shot in the back when I was lying down because of the laws of physics. But I felt as if I had actually been shot. My first reaction was sorrow at leaving my kids and my family and my life—I thought I was dying and assumed that's why everything seemed so weird and unreal. Then I realized I was still in bed, and I felt a surge of hope that maybe I hadn't died after all. I could still see inside my body and view the bone fragments from my spine, and my next concern was that I was paralyzed. I tried wiggling my toes, and when I was able to, I was so relieved I started to cry. That was the end of the experience. The walls of our bedroom reappeared from the ground up, and my perception returned to normal. I got out of bed because I was so rattled. I went and looked out the kitchen window into our back yard. Everything looked exactly like it was supposed to look. I wondered if the experience was some sort of premonition or a past-life memory or if stress was just driving me toward a nervous breakdown.

Many years later, I learned from the Peter Tompkins book *The Secret Life of Nature* that there is a form of astral vision that describes the strange simultaneous, multiple-perspective vision I had that night. In his book, Tompkins tells about a form of astral vision that the Theosophists referred to by the quaint if clunky term "withinth." Tompkins describes this particular type of astral vision as "a sort of four-dimensional sense of seeing an object from all sides at once and from inside as well." Tompkins reveals that with astral sight, a person can see "equally well behind and beneath" an object without turning their head. I also learned from this book that the initial experience of seeing my bedroom walls melt away was a similar form of perception that the Theosophists referred to as etheric vision. According to Tompkins, "Etheric vision is described [by Theosophists] as 'throughth,' meaning the ability to see through opaque objects." Another fascinating thing the Theosophists believed is that by using etheric sight, people could see the "denser etheric bodies of the lower orders of nature spirits" such as fairies, gnomes, and brownies. Using more refined astral sight, people can perceive practically anything, from subatomic particles (electrons and atoms) to radiant water nymphs. Perhaps Molly and her cousin Jill were tuned in to the etheric realm when they saw the tiny barefoot people in Molly's room.

A few years before we moved out of Wisconsin, I started to read a lot of books on metaphysical topics and talked to my kids about what I was discovering. My parents had some books on Edgar Cayce, the sleeping clairvoyant from the 1930s. Cayce, who was brought up in a relatively conservative Southern Christian home, had started out doing self-hypnosis for healing. He moved on to doing healing readings for other people and eventually started to explore topics such as reincarnation and life on other planets while in a trance state. I also read the works of Ruth Montgomery, a respected Washington, D. C., political columnist who had written a book about Jeane Dixon before writing a series of channeled books using automatic writing. Edgar Cayce and Ruth Montgomery's traditional backgrounds and mainstream lives added credibility to the metaphysical concepts they explored that, at the time, were unfamiliar and vaguely threatening to me.

When Jack was a teenager, he decided to have an out-of-body experience. He felt himself lifting out of his body feet-first, which he said felt really cool. Then he opened his eyes a crack to see if he was really leaving his body. He felt a jolt of raw fear when he saw a dark, human-shaped silhouette lifting him out of his body. Jack was staying with some friends of ours when this happened, sleeping in a makeshift basement bedroom. He got so freaked out that he had to go get the husband to come and sleep on the other spare bed in the basement so he wouldn't be downstairs alone.

· · · · · ·

One of the metaphysical books I read while living in Hudson told how to hypnotize people so that they could meet their spirit guide. My sister Maggie was in between traveling adventures and was staying with us for a while. She and Molly agreed to be hypnotized. They lay down on the living room floor, which was carpeted but still not that comfortable. I droned on (in what I thought was a hypnotic voice) through a lengthy script that went on for several pages. Neither Molly nor Maggie was laughing, so I thought they might actually be having a cool astral journey. Eventually, we got to the part where I brought them out of their hypnotic state. I got nervous when I couldn't get either one of them to become unhypnotized, so I shook them a little bit to try and wake them up. It turned out they had both fallen sound asleep, and neither Maggie nor Molly was very happy about being woken up. When I asked them if they had met their spirit guides, Maggie said she couldn't remember anything at all. Molly said she met her spirit guide and he looked like Jon Bon Jovi.

When the kids were in junior high school, there was a period of time in Hudson that we had a Ouija board in the house again. I can't remember where it came from, although I would guess either the kids asked for one and I relented or they just got one from someplace and brought it in. Anyway, they were told only to use it when I was home and to do a small protection prayer before beginning each session. The kids did not have any dramatic Ouija board experiences that I ever heard about except for one, which had them both in tears before it was over.

When Jack was in grade school, my sister Iris had three kittens to give away. We already had David Grey Hair, who had basically adopted Molly as his companion human, so Jack got to choose a kitten. He chose a sweet and energetic little white kitten with black spots and named him Frisky. Frisky had some developmental challenges, but that just made him even more endearing. He was really good-natured and completely guileless, unlike David Grey Hair, who was smart and sneaky and complicated. Our cats were indoor and outdoor cats in those days, and when Frisky was four or five years old, I started to notice him behaving strangely. For example, I'd see him sitting off by himself in unusual places—on the front steps (where he had never hung out before) or on the compost heap beside the garage. One day, I found our friendly and active Frisky sitting all alone in the corner of the basement. I picked him up to pet him, and my heart sank. Frisky was so light, he felt empty. The weight loss had happened within the space of just a few weeks. I made an appointment with the vet the next day. I did not have a good feeling about Frisky's health. Now that we were really focused on him, Frisky seemed uncharacteristically vacant. It was like he wasn't even in his body anymore. In the morning, I wrapped Frisky in a big blanket to take him to the vet. I felt like I was carrying a shell of our kitty. Jack was so crushed, he didn't want to come out of his room. I said, "Jack, you have to come and say goodbye to Frisky. You might not see him again."

Jack came out of his room, completely broken up. And—I wouldn't have believed this if I hadn't been holding Frisky in my arms and seen it up close—Frisky's spirit came back into his body to say goodbye to Jack. A moment earlier, Frisky had looked and felt like an empty shell. His eyes were open but looked completely blank. But when Jack approached him, Frisky became present and real. He looked at Jack with love as Jack told him goodbye. Then Frisky was gone again. By this time, we were all crying. The vet tested Frisky and discovered he had feline leukemia, which was something we had never heard of at the time. We had to put Frisky to sleep; there was no choice. We had a small memorial service in which we scattered Frisky's ashes in his favorite spot in the yard and played the Ray Charles song "I Can't Stop Loving You."

Some time after Frisky's death, the kids were consulting the Ouija board and had asked for a friendly spirit to come through. The planchette started to move, and when they asked who the spirit was, it spelled out FRISKY. They got very quiet. Then one of the kids asked, "Where are you, Frisky?" and the board spelled out HEVN, which seems like exactly how Frisky would spell heaven. That's when the kids both got completely choked up.

In 1994, we moved out of our occasionally quirky little house in Hudson, Wisconsin, trading up from a weirdness standpoint to a house full of ghosts in Sibley, Minnesota.

*Me and my siblings, circa 1967. Left to right, back row: me,
Maggie, Iris, and Betsy; front row: Thomas, Dan, and Randall.*

To the outside world we all grow old. But not to brothers and sisters. We know each other as we always were… We remember family feuds and secrets, family griefs and joys. We live outside the touch of time.

Clara Ortega

The Laughing Boy and the Girl in the Glass: Stories from My Brothers and Sisters

On Christmas Eve a few years ago, my parents and most of my siblings and our kids were sitting around the dining room table. We were eating a roast beef dinner, with spinach lasagna for the young vegetarians among us, and speculating with my youngest nieces and nephews what time Santa would arrive and what presents he might bring. When the doorbell rang, we all yelled out, "Hi George!" or "Merry Christmas, George!" because nearly every Christmas since he died, my mom's dog George stops by and rings the doorbell. My mom can see spirits—not all the time, but more than any of the rest of us can. She has seen George's spirit several times since he died, playing with the kids in the sunken living room, trotting into the sunroom, sometimes even jumping into her lap. George was in pretty bad shape when he died, but whenever my mom sees him, he is healthy and fit. The doorbell usually rings once before my mom sees George's spirit, and we consider the doorbell to be George's signature greeting. So on Christmas Eve when the doorbell rang a second time, we were all surprised. Someone got up and looked out the window and said, "Oh, the UPS man is here." It hadn't occurred to any of us that it might be a human being in a physical body at the door. We all laughed as my brother's girlfriend Lila said, "You guys know you're weird, right?"

So, in the spirit of weirdness and in honor of Lila, here are some of the ghostly or supernatural experiences my siblings have had that weren't covered in other chapters.

Iris

My older sister, Iris, is fierce and smart. When we were growing up, she wrote plays for us younger kids to perform and (I was so envious of this) could play the accordion. She had two accordions, a big one and a small one, and the rest of us weren't allowed to touch them.

Iris had the really cool experience of seemingly being transported backwards in time when we lived in Ottawa. Iris is four years older than I am, so she was eleven or younger when this happened. It was a sunny summer day and she was walking out to the clothesline with a basket of laundry to hang on the line. Iris said that, as she walked, she got distracted by the pattern of dappled shadows moving on the ground caused by sunlight shining through swaying tree branches. She saw a fire pit, and as she knelt down for a closer look, she suddenly realized that instead of her own bare feet and legs, she was wearing moccasins and suede leggings. The fire pit, with the cold remains of the previous night's fire, was in a dried creek bed. Lying in the cold ashes was a bone that looked like an animal's leg joint, with meat still on it. When Iris picked up the bone to take it with her, she saw that the meat was partially raw. She got disgusted and threw the bone back into the fire pit. Iris's strong emotional reaction to the raw meat seemed to break the vision, and suddenly, everything was back to normal.

Iris said that when she was seeing the fire pit scene, it felt normal. She felt like she was a Native American man who was preparing to leave the spot where he had camped the night before. She didn't feel like she was herself trapped in an alternate reality or anything. Iris thought the experience might be a past-life memory. Another possibility is that the moving pattern of light triggered a change in consciousness, and Iris tuned in to a scene from the past associated with the land itself. Our house was built on land that had been Dakota/Sioux territory a little more than a hundred years earlier.

Thomas

My dark-eyed older brother Thomas, who inherited our Montana cowboy relatives' love of horses and the West, is sort of a mad genius who coined words and phrases such as "snorkafueny, fueny, fueny," which he mumbled when he was pretending to be asleep to keep pesky younger siblings away. Thomas doesn't eat candy, which gave him a terrible power over the rest of us. He kept his share of whatever candy we got in his underwear drawer so no one would steal it, and he used his candy stash to bribe us or as rewards in his twisted magnum opus, Quiet Game. The goal of Quiet Game was to progress through a series of designated stations in the living room by being the quietest person in the room, as determined by Thomas. Meanwhile, he would stand in the center of the living room and watch us, occasionally telling jokes to try to make us laugh. Sometimes after telling a joke, he would say, "You may laugh." But just as often as not, he'd follow this magnanimous gesture with a quick "Stop!" Anyone who couldn't stop giggling had to move back one station. As far as paranormal experiences, Thomas says he has had none. Ghosts probably couldn't top anything Thomas could come up with anyway.

Betsy

When she was a kid, my younger sister Betsy was nicknamed Betsy Brown Eyes because of her big brown eyes. As a child, Betsy was really shy and really smart. She has had more paranormal experiences than most of my other siblings, especially out-of-body experiences, or OBEs.

One of Betsy's first successful astral projection experiences came after she took a class on astral projection through the local chapter of Open U. Betsy had often experienced incomplete OBEs in the past, in which she felt her astral body lifting out of her physical body feet first, but not making it all the way out, usually getting stuck at her head before she was jolted awake. (Lifting out feet first is the way I most often experience OBEs, too.) After the Open U class, Betsy lifted all the way out of her body. She wanted to connect with our grandma Dorrie, but the first spirit she saw was a young girl crying in the corner of her bedroom. The girl had long dark braids and was wearing a white nightgown and seemed both unhappy and out of sorts. (More on this odd similarity with my mom's ghost girl in a minute.) Betsy recalls having a brief conversation with the girl to try to find out why she was unhappy but does not remember getting any real answer, and moved on. Our grandma Dorrie was present in this astral experience, sitting at Betsy's kitchen table with our Montana grandma, Grandma Morgan. But it was our Montana teddy-bear grandpa, Grandpa Morgan, who was the most animated and interactive spirit in this experience. In her OBE, Betsy saw our grandpa Morgan at the end of the long hall, by the doorway to her kitchen. She flew down the hallway and into his arms. She said she felt Grandpa Morgan's love and reassurance.

Betsy said she was able to ask Grandpa Morgan a few questions, which he answered. She can't remember that part of the conversation anymore, a situation she finds completely annoying. She does remember that when she asked our grandpa if dead people could watch what's happening on earth, she had a sense she had gone too far. All of our grandparents disappeared, and Betsy flew back down to her bedroom and somersaulted into her body.

I just learned the detail of the little crying girl's dark braids and white nightgown as I was fact-checking Betsy's experience while writing this chapter. (She had this OBE before my mom had discovered the identity of the ghost girl who followed her around.) Betsy is certain this little girl was not part of her own spirit. Did Betsy, like Randall, tune in to my mom's ghost girl? I'm inclined to say no, just because neither my mom nor my brother Randall perceived the ghost girl as unhappy. That leads me to wonder why four of us in our family have seen a ghost girl in a long white nightgown. I do feel confident that my mom perceived part of her own spirit. And since Randall saw the same ghost girl hanging around my mom, I believe he also saw my mom's ghost girl. The true identity of the ghost girl I saw while brushing my teeth at my grandparents' house is less certain, but because I saw her in my mom's childhood home, I think there's a good likelihood that she was associated with my mom. But Betsy saw her ghost girl in her own home and displaying different behavior than the girl that Randall and I saw. Maybe a ghost girl is sometimes just an archetype, like the ubiquitous hitchhiker ghost or crying baby spirit.

One of my worst nightmares, which I had as an adult, was of being trapped in Grandma and Grandpa Haraldson's house. The dream had an "off" vibe from the very beginning and quickly became very disturbing. In the dream, I knew my grandparents had both already died and there was no reason for me to be there. Their house was eerily empty, but as soon as I realized how odd that was, random pieces of furniture started to materialize around me. This completely freaked me out, since it seemed like something sentient was both aware of my thoughts and trying deliberately to mislead me. At the beginning of the dream, Molly and I had gone to my grandparent's house to clean, but at some point, Molly disappeared. I started calling for her, knowing the house was bewitched and we had to get out. I knew somehow that Molly had gone upstairs, and I went to get her. I had to run past a possessed man sitting in a chair in the front hallway. He was in the throes of violent seizures but turned to look at me as I ran past, and his eyes were twirling patterns. It was then I realized that something evil had taken over his body. When I got to the top of the staircase, I hollered for Molly. Instead of Molly, Betsy came out of one of the upstairs rooms. She was about six years old, was wearing a white nightgown, and had no feet. The dream ended there because I woke up.

The other weird coincidence about all this is that in one of Betsy's OBEs (which she experienced before hearing anything about my nightmare), she felt like she was floating in darkness in some sort of clear membrane bubble. She could see young girls in white nightgowns floating in other bubbles, and none of the girls had feet.

Betsy's psychic experiences continued after her daughter Christine was born. Christine was a very light sleeper, and like all new parents, Betsy was pretty sleep-deprived. One day, Betsy was drinking a glass of water and wondering if she had the energy necessary to take care of a baby. When Betsy lifted up the glass of water to take another sip, she saw Christine's smiling face looking up at her from the bottom of the glass! Betsy thought she must be seeing things because she was so tired, but when she looked again, Christine's face was still there, smiling up at her. Betsy took this as a message that everything was going to be fine.

I love the smiling baby Christine story. I think being sleep-deprived put Betsy in a state of consciousness in which she did some spontaneous scrying. Scrying is the age-old art of seeing the future or gaining insight into current situations by gazing into a reflective surface such as a pool of water or a mirror and interpreting the images you see. I think the way scrying works can be explained by something I read once: You are a spirit, you have a body. I believe we exist in the physical world and spirit world simultaneously, and that we have access to an unlimited pool of information if we can find a technique for bypassing the limitations of our conscious mind. Done properly, scrying does just that.

Christine had a dramatic psychic experience as a toddler. Betsy had an extremely long and difficult labor with Christine. After forty-nine hours of labor and some complications during the delivery process, the doctors delivered Christine by cesarean section. When Betsy got home from the hospital, she put the bathrobe she had worn during labor—a distinctive, brightly flowered silk robe—in the back of her closet.

One morning when Christine was just over two years old, Betsy wore the robe while preparing breakfast. It was the first time she had worn it since being in the hospital. Christine stared very long and hard at the robe when she first saw it but said nothing. As Betsy fed Christine her breakfast, Christine said, "Mama, the baby wants to get out. The baby wants to get out now. The baby wants to get out NOW!"

When I heard this story, my guess was that Christine was spontaneously practicing psychometry, or in other words, reading the highly charged energy imbued in the bathrobe. Betsy's first thought was that Christine might have had an out-of-body experience during delivery because of all the physical and emotional stress of the labor, and was watching "the baby" trying to be born from an observer's point of view. On a few occasions, Christine has demonstrated the ability to tune in to Betsy's thoughts, commenting specifically on dilemmas that Betsy was pondering, usually involving how to handle stressful social situations. Christine is now seven years old, smart and shy like her mom and a writer of spooky stories like her aunt Annie.

Randall

My younger brother Randall has always been tall, athletic, and exceptionally easygoing. In fact, he was so mellow that in many of the pictures we have of him as a child, he's sound asleep—either that or he's tromping around in his cowboy boots with his equally mellow and oversized cat Big Black under his arm. He and his wife Karen live in California. For a while after they were married, they lived together in Karen's house, and they both have had ghost experiences there. Karen's parents own the house, and they believe there are three ghosts that visit occasionally, and that the ghosts are the spirits of the people who first owned the property.

Karen said the ghost activity usually involved hearing loud cracking and popping noises, especially in one particular corner, that neither she nor Randall could explain, tapping sounds as though something was tapping on a piece of wood, doors opening on their own, and doorknobs and windows jiggling. The spirits liked to play with a metal dragon that Karen had hanging on the wall, moving it from side to side and making small noises with it. Occasionally the spirits would help her out. If Karen set her alarm and didn't get up, they would make a racket until she got out of bed. One night, a friend who didn't believe in ghosts spent the night at their house. He woke up because he heard someone calling his name. It was a woman, so he assumed it was Karen. But Karen had been asleep and in her room with Randall all night, so they concluded it must have been a ghost.

Karen said the only time she was really scared was when she was home alone and heard heavy footsteps walking up the hallway toward her. Randall suggested she tell the spirits to stop making noises because it scared her. She did, and the noises stopped. However, when Randall came into their room one night, he saw a woman in a white diaphanous gown standing beside their bed, watching Karen sleep. They moved out of the house a few years ago. (Karen reports that the dragon decoration is hanging on the wall at their new place, and has neither moved nor made a sound.) She and Randall do not know if the people who are now living in their former house have met the original owners or not.

Maggie

My younger sister Maggie is the adventurous one of our family. She has always had an outgoing personality, and as a kid, her warm nature and winning smile made her pretty much completely adorable. As an adult, Maggie has traveled extensively and has lived in both Spain and India. Maggie had a time-anomaly experience similar to Iris's while she was living in Seville, Spain. She had gone to explore some Roman ruins with her friends. At the time, Maggie was standing by herself in what remained of a city. All that was left were the foundations of houses, low stone walls, and some tiles. The layouts of the rooms and location of where some of the chimneys had been were still visible in some of the homes. Maggie was wondering what the place had been like when it was a city when suddenly, the scene changed, and it was a city. There were people everywhere, apparently just going about their daily business. No one took any notice of Maggie at all. She watched the hustle and bustle of the people, and like Iris, she didn't feel scared or lost in time. It felt very normal. She felt like she belonged in the scene until she looked down and saw her modern-day sundress. Maggie's first impression was that she wasn't dressed right. Then the true scope of the experience hit her, and the scene disappeared. Maggie said it was so powerful and moving that she had tears running down her face afterward. For many years, she assumed this was a past-life flashback, but now she thinks it could also have been a "wrinkle in time" kind of bleed-through.

Maggie also had two out-of-body experiences while in high school, both precipitated by doing aerobic workouts to her Joanie Greggains record (a collection of '80s pop songs). Our sister Betsy learned in a class on OBEs that the ideal state for experiencing astral travel was when your body was relaxed and your mind alert, which accurately describes Maggie's post-aerobics state. Unfortunately, Maggie had never heard of astral projection when the OBEs happened and thought she was going crazy. Maggie's first OBE happened when she was zoning out on the couch right after exercising. She said her eyes were open, but she wasn't focused on anything. A song from the Joanie Greggains record was going through her mind when suddenly, the song she was thinking of speeded up, as if someone were playing a 33 rpm record at 45 rpm. What happened next was that Maggie found herself (or at least found her awareness and visual perspective) in three separate places in our parents' house in quick progression. Our mom was in the kitchen frying bacon, and first, Maggie had the perspective of being inside the frying pan. Next, she found herself in the midst of our younger brothers Dan and Sam's informal wrestling match in the sunken living room. Her last impression was of being directly in front of the television screen in the sunroom. That's when Maggie got scared and wondered what was happening. As soon as she felt fear, she found herself back on the couch, perceiving the people and events around her in the usual way.

Maggie's second OBE was in the shower, again shortly after she had finished working out. One minute she was in the shower, and the next thing she knew, she was watching a woman wash her arm. She was viewing it from above and slightly to the left, and at first she didn't realize she was looking at herself. Maggie said, "As soon as I realized it was ME I was seeing, I was back inside my body." She said she was startled to discover that, while viewing herself washing her arm, she couldn't feel any sensation at all. In other words, she perceived herself visually but not in a tactile way.

I think Maggie's experience of not being able to perceive the physical sensation of washing her arm while having an OBE adds credence to my belief that OBEs are either a form of dissociation or operate on the same principle. (Dissociation is a medically recognized state of consciousness in which people perceive themselves as being outside their own physical body, usually as a coping mechanism in response to extreme trauma, like torture or abuse.) Maggie did say that the OBEs happened during one of the most stressful times in her life. I think dissociation is related to the phenomenon of soul loss, as well.

Maggie's husband Rob is a musician who has occasional intuitive flashes, like the time recently when he had a foreboding sense of death in their neighborhood. He found out later there had been a murder on their block the previous night. When Rob and Maggie were living in Bangalore, India, they had a weird haunting experience. The company Maggie worked for had leased a huge mansion for its employees to share and staffed it with a cook and an assistant cook; additional staff included a gardener, a housekeeper, a driver, and a security guard. Large residences in India are often named, and their house was called Sampradaya. Three single women, Maggie's coworkers, lived at Sampradaya as well. Each person or couple had a private bedroom and bathroom, and shared a common dining room and kitchen. The company let employees live in the house rent-free as part of their compensation.

Maggie and Rob and the other women lived in the house for nearly a year without incident. Then the haunting commenced. While in India, Maggie and Rob sent out an email newsletter, the "Bangalore Chronicles," about their experiences to all of their family and friends. Here is Rob's account of the haunting.

BANGALORE CHRONICLES, JUNE 23, 2001

*Which brings me to the recent episode of "household mass hysteria" that gripped the residents of our guesthouse for several weeks last month. Valerie, Jo, Ivy and Maggie (who sleep in separate rooms) all reported a number of incidents where they were awakened around 4 AM by rappings on the door, door handles being jiggled, whisperings, and such. Through subsequent investigations, we ruled out the possibility of house staff being responsible, and then of outside intruders who may have broken in at night. That's when a "supernatural" explanation started to uneasily gain some steam. And the noises, the rappings, continued—always at the bewitching hour of 4 AM. I even set my alarm one night at 3:55 and laid in wait for whatever might come, but (as is often the fate of the skeptic) I saw nothing. What finally pushed the experience over the edge of normalcy and into the freak-out zone was something that Sampad†
let slip out of the bag. That these visits were NOT unusual and that they were from "witches"—ghost spirits of young Indian women who had killed themselves for one reason or another, and now were making regular nocturnal visits to the young single women in the house. Not to harm them, but just to bug them.*

Dilbag‡ revealed that he had twice seen them floating in the trees late at night behind the house. One of the guards related a story to Sampad that was especially creepy. He said that one night he dozed off—and when awakened, he discovered that he was being carried.

---

† The cook.
‡ The assistant cook.

He shook himself to his senses, and found himself standing in the middle of the yard being stared at by four young women—who then just sort of dissipated into the ether. You can imagine how comforting all these stories were to the single women of the house. (Although I'm still not sure why Maggie heard something one night—perhaps I should double-check the validity of our marriage license.)

Anyway, to wrap things up, the noises have stopped. Things are once again back to normal at Sampradaya. But! As an extremely interesting footnote: one night Jo and Ivy returned to the house from a wedding. They had gone all-out with the Indian dress thing: full saris, strings of jasmine in their hair, and bindis (the forehead dot). So they took a picture of themselves. Ivy held the camera and shot the two of them standing framed in an ornate downstairs mirror. The developed picture caused quite a stir. There are three faces in the photo! Jo's, Ivy's, and then a distinctly ghoulish, scary countenance peering over Jo's shoulder. Folks, it's positively freakazoidal. We would have sent the photo along with this edition of the Bang Chrons, but Jo's holding off on major distribution until she sees if there's any chance to market this baby to the National Enquirer.

Whatever it all means (and I'm sure the truth is out there), it does point out how closely the Hindu mind links the spirit and material worlds. None of this appears to be too out of the ordinary to Sampad and Dilbag.

The staff suggested that Maggie, Rob, and the single women put up pictures of a common Indian protection gargoyle (surprisingly, not a god or goddess) on their bedroom doors to keep the witches away. They all did this, and the rattling of the doorknobs ceased. (See the photo gallery for photos of both the ghost face and the protection gargoyle.)

· · · · · ·

Back in the United States, Maggie and Rob both noticed an increase in astral experiences after their twin sons, Oscar and Carter, were born. Actually, when Maggie discovered she was pregnant, I asked her if she had any inkling as to whether she was having a boy or a girl. Maggie said she didn't have any feeling as to the baby's gender, but whenever she thought about her baby, she thought of "them" rather than him or her. She found out when she was further along that she was expecting twins.

Rob says he considers himself a skeptic about paranormal experiences who is willing to be proven wrong. He says the following experience was one of the first in his life that seemed unexplainable, although three and a half years later, he's not sure anymore if it was paranormal or just messed-up perception due to sleep deprivation. One night, when the boys were babies, Rob woke up. He saw a silhouette of Maggie standing in the hallway comforting one of the babies in her arms. Then he rolled over and saw Maggie asleep in bed next to him. Upon seeing Maggie, he quickly looked back to the hall and found it empty. He was completely freaked out. At that point, he dashed into Oscar and Carter's bedroom, fully expecting to find an intruder, but found only the boys asleep. Then he quickly called Maggie and woke her up. He continued to frantically search the house for someone until it became clear there was no one there.

Another night, Maggie woke up in the middle of the night because she heard one of the boys laughing. Rob woke up when Maggie did. He hadn't heard anything, but he saw one of the boys standing in the nursery, having climbed out of his crib. I think it's interesting that both Maggie and Rob perceived one of their children but in completely different ways—Rob visually and Maggie in an auditory way. Rob quickly got up to put whichever twin it was (they couldn't tell for sure) back in his crib, but in the six seconds it took Rob to reach the nursery, he found both boys asleep in their cribs. This happened at a time when the twins could scarcely climb out of their cribs, let alone climb back in by themselves. No laughing little boy was anywhere to be found.

Sleep deprivation has been used as a vision-inducing technique in initiation and healing rituals for ages. I think, in the latter case, Maggie and Rob's new parent sleep-deprivation acted as a doorway to perceiving

Oscar or Carter's astral form, out of his crib and exploring the nursery at night. As for the first experience, Rob doesn't know who the woman was.

Other than possibly making the unexpected appearance in the hallway, Carter has not had any paranormal experiences that we are aware of. He loves solving mysteries and telling stories, and is always on the lookout for interesting and weird events. Oscar's natural skills include a highly developed sense of empathy and insight. He had a very interesting dream about a mean elf who lives in a violin that we are going to use as the main character in a story.

Dan

My brother Dan, whose girlfriend Lila is the one this chapter is dedicated to, has had two paranormal experiences that he can't explain. Dan was a remarkably cute kid who from a young age demonstrated a fierce independent streak that you might not expect to see in someone with six older siblings. Unfortunately, neither of Dan's ghostly experiences was very positive. In the first, he had been working outside in the heat (he works as a homebuilder) and had come home to take a shower and get cleaned up before going out. He lay down on his bed for a few minutes and fell asleep. He woke up because he heard a strange crackling noise. He looked around and saw a bright ball of golden light floating near the ceiling. Dan was trying to figure out what the light could be when it suddenly zapped him! He said it felt like he was getting a shock. The shock lasted for a long time—nearly thirty seconds, by Dan's estimation. Then the light disappeared. Dan rented this house out for a while to a man from Ireland, who apparently had a different kind of weird experience there. The Irish man asked Dan if the house had brownies. (Brownies are helpful—but capricious—house fairies.) Dan thought the renter was joking, but he wasn't. He told Dan that someone was straightening out the shoes and boots piled by the door each night, which is exactly the kind of tidying-up behavior brownies are known to exhibit.

Believe it or not, Dan's other paranormal experience was even worse—I refer to it as the time he got beat up by a ghost, although he likes to remind me that technically, he only got pinned down, and therefore the scuffle ended in a draw, with no clear winner.

Between doing construction work, running, biking, and kayaking, Dan is in exceptionally good shape. But when he had surgery on an old rotator cuff injury, the doctors told him he had to have someone around to help him out for the first few days after surgery. Since Lila works full time, Dan went to stay at our parents' house. My parents have plenty of ghost activity at their house, but their ghost has never hurt anyone— until Dan spent the night. He was sleeping in the recliner because it was more comfortable than trying to lie down on his sore shoulder. Dan said he woke up because he felt something pin him down. One of the main spirits at my mom and dad's house is a male ghost who sometimes smells like cigarette smoke, but all the ghost usually does is walk up the staircase or make his way down the hallway toward the bedrooms. He also bangs around in whatever rooms my mom and dad aren't in.

After realizing he was being held down, Dan tried to hit whoever had him pinned. He was at a disadvantage since he couldn't see anyone, was in a lot of pain, and his good arm was in a sling. Eventually, the ghost just disappeared. I have no idea why a spirit would try to beat up my brother, although I do enjoy razzing him about it from time to time. Dan always reminds me he was on painkillers when it happened. And I always remind him that most people on painkillers don't get accosted by ghosts.

Sam

My youngest brother, Sam, is ten years younger than I am, so when he was little, my girlfriends and I liked to play with him and pretend he was our baby. Sam had big blue eyes, dark blond hair, and a serious nature. He now works as a soil-testing engineer, so it seems fitting that his only unusual experience—which may or may not have been an OBE

—is his story of getting smacked down into the ground by "the big hand of God."

Sam characterizes the experience as an unusually vivid dream in which he felt himself flying out of his body. Sam said it felt really cool, like he was flying at high speed straight up into the sky. He was completely unafraid, even as he left the earth's atmosphere and entered outer space. All of a sudden, a huge hand appeared out of nowhere. He heard a male voice boom NO! as the hand smacked him down. Sam said he hurtled backwards to Earth and hit the ground so hard he was actually embedded in the dirt. He does remember thinking, "Is this a dream?" Sam does not usually have lucid dreams, so even that aspect of the dream was unusual.

Sam's wife, Jenny, is vivacious and petite, and used to be a defense free safety for the Minnesota Vixen, a team in the Independent Women's Football League. She lived in a haunted house in California from the time she was a baby until she was almost three, when her parents moved back to Minnesota. As a toddler, she was terrified of something in her room. One night, Jenny asked her mom for water. When her mom came back with it, Jenny came running out of her room screaming and crying. For the next few days, Jenny would peer around the door before entering her room and was very tentative about going inside, but whatever had been in there seemed to be gone. Jenny's mom came to believe the house was haunted too. She would hear footsteps on the carpet behind her, but no one was there when she turned around. But at least one of the spirits in the California house was helpful. A ghost woke up Jenny's mom one night when Jenny had thrown her blanket on the space heater, so she was able to remove it before it caused a fire. Another time, when her mom was really sick, Jenny's dad woke up and saw an old woman kneeling beside the bed, praying for her. Jenny's mom had never talked to her husband about the ghost because she didn't think he'd believe her. He became a believer anyway when he woke up one night, being pulled off the bed by something he couldn't see. He yelled for Jenny's mom to help him, saying, "Hold on to me, hold on to me! Something is pulling me out of the bed!" Jenny's mom grabbed onto him, and whatever it was went away.

Sam and Jenny have two daughters, Mahala, age four, and Ava, age one. Ava is a fearless go-getter with a ready smile—or growl—depending on what the situation calls for. We will have to wait until Ava is a little older to hear her stories.

Mahala is smart and serious and sweet. One night when Jenny was reading bedtime stories to her, Mahala kept looking up at the ceiling in the corner of her room. Jenny finally asked her what she was looking at. She wasn't expecting Mahala to answer, "The old lady in a chair in the air." Mahala asked Jenny to make the old lady go away. Jenny told Mahala that she couldn't see the old lady, but she still told the old lady to go away. Jenny also told Mahala to let her know if she saw the old lady again because no one should be in her room that made her uncomfortable. With the youngest members of our families we try to strike a balance, both listening to what they're saying and making sure they feel safe and secure. Jenny did a blessing and protection ritual for the room to keep the energy clear.

More recently, Mahala was at my parents' house and casually remarked, "I had a different mom once."

My mom, caught completely off-guard, replied, "You did?"

"Yeah," said Mahala. "But she went away or something. I don't remember ..." Mahala also told my mom that, when she grows up, she's going to change her name to Emily, "because that's my real name." After this bit of commentary, Mahala just started playing again. Mahala's comment is especially interesting because as far as we know, she has not been exposed to the concept of reincarnation. There has been some really compelling research done on children remembering past lives. Dr. Ian Stevenson conducted extensive studies, primarily in India. Reincarnation is a central tenet of Hinduism, the dominant religion in India, and therefore parents there pay attention to their children's past-life memories. Dr. Stevenson found that children were most likely to remember past lives before age seven. One of the fascinating things that

Dr. Stevenson discovered is that if someone died tragically, some evidence of how they died will often appear on their physical body in their next incarnation in the form of a scar or birthmark.

Sophia

My sister Iris's daughter Sophia is an artist and photographer who has a particular affinity for nature spirits. When she was fifteen, she saw green, glowing lights in her bedroom at night. On various occasions throughout that entire summer, Sophia woke up at night and noticed different objects or parts of objects glowing green when her room was dark. The first was the lower parts of some spines of books on her bookshelf, then it was part of a shelf on the wall or a spot on the wall. Another time it was just the leg of a wooden chair near her bed. When Sophia turned the light on, everything looked normal; when she turned it off, the objects would glow again. She didn't sense anything bad from the green glow, but she was spooked enough to leave the light on when she slept, most of the time. Sophia said it was a pretty intense time in her life and that it may have been related to excess emotional energy. She did an experiment to see if the green light had left residual energy in her room, putting one of her plants on the shelf where she'd seen the glowing light, but a move to the glowing light spot didn't seem to affect the plant in any noticeable way.

Gwendolyn

Iris's younger daughter, Gwendolyn, is whip-smart, focused, and very giving of her time and talent. Gwendolyn was the youngest grandchild for quite a few years and has spent lots of time at my house. The last time she spent the night, a few years ago, Gwendolyn heard footsteps upstairs, then she heard someone clear his throat right in front of her. (She was standing by the clock in the kitchen at the time.) Weirdly, when Gwendolyn told my mom about it the next day, my mom said she had heard someone clearing his throat at their house the night before! My mom had never heard that particular ghost noise at her house before. It's possible that my mom was actually tuned in to Gwendolyn's experience, rather than hearing a spirit at her own house. I find these random shared family paranormal experiences to be comforting. It's like we're all so in tune with each other, we have a collective family energy field to rely on if we need a hand.

That same night Gwendolyn heard someone clearing his throat, she had a nightmare that scared her enough that she came and slept in my room. Gwendolyn's dream involved a diabolical female ghost with a shaved head—the same dream character Molly had dreamt about a decade earlier that scared Molly so much she came and slept in my bed. Gwendolyn was sleeping in the guest room. She dreamt that I came into her room and said I wanted to show her something. I looked toward the wall and it started to move and shift. It morphed into a blank wall. The closet door disappeared. Gwendolyn and I could see right through the wall, and there was a ghost in the otherwise empty closet. It was the shaved-head ghost from Molly's nightmare. Gwendolyn said the ghost had an angry expression on her face and seemed evil. She was sitting in a bluish-gray recliner. Gwendolyn was terrified. She said it didn't feel like I was in the room anymore, but it seemed as if Leon, our protective house spirit, was there. Then the shaved-head ghost's expression changed, and she seemed less threatening, almost sorrowful. That's when Gwendolyn woke up. Gwendolyn had heard the story of Molly's nightmare, so it is entirely possible Molly's dream was on her mind when she went to bed. But what I found compelling was the chair in which the ghost was sitting. Gwendolyn had no way of knowing that the bluish-gray recliner has been in both an OBE that I had and part of a creative visualization exercise that I had done several times. In my OBE, I was actually sitting in the chair. I remember thinking how ridiculous it was to be sitting in a recliner while astral projecting, and that ended the experience. It was the only time I've felt self-conscious during an OBE. In the creative visualization exercise, I imagined myself going to a quiet room and sitting in a comfortable chair. I pictured a big screen in the room, and basically projected a movie of my intended goal coming true on the screen. I always imagined a bluish-gray recliner as the comfortable chair. I stopped doing this exercise after a while because it seemed to me like it was just as effective to do what I've always done to reach my goals: decide what I want to accomplish and then go for it. I am usually picturing what I want in my mind, just because that's how I'm wired, rather than using it as a deliberate technique. I have read in various magical books that people should take the time to dispose of things they've created on the astral realm (usually referred to as "thought forms"). Otherwise, it's like being an astral litterbug. There is a theory that thought forms that are magical in origin (created through willpower) can even take on a life of their own. A sentient thought form is known as a tulpa.

Levi

A person doesn't have to believe in ghosts to fit into our family, but I was happy to learn that my beau Levi had a supernatural experience in his childhood. He was a farm kid in Illinois and was staying at a friend's house overnight. He and his friend were helping with farm chores. When they were walking back across the farmyard after chores, they heard a loud clanging noise from over beside one of the outbuildings, and when they went to investigate, they saw that the sound had come from a bunch of metal milk cans stored there. They didn't see anything that could have made such a loud and sustained clanging—no cat could have done it, and there were no dogs around, but they shrugged it off and went inside for supper. Later that evening, after dark, they were out in the barn, sitting around on the hay bales, when they both got a strange feeling and decided to go back to the house. They latched the barn door behind them and had started across the barnyard when they heard a banging noise from the door. When they turned to look, they saw the barn door moving and banging like someone or something was inside trying very hard to get out. Levi says the distance from the barn to the house has probably never been covered as fast before or since. When they got to Levi's friend's bedroom on the second floor, they peeked out the window over to the barnyard and saw the barn door open, swinging back and forth. As they were looking at the door and talking about what could have possibly opened it from the inside or been strong enough to break it, they saw a moving shadow in front of the white wooden fence between the house and barn. The shadow was larger than a man, upright, and moving in a strange, furtive, almost animal-like way. Levi said he and his friend never did discover what came out of the barn that night.

. . . . . .

This past year, our family had a very simple Christmas celebration, reflecting both the world's economic situation and my mom's recovery from surgery earlier in the month. We focused on spending the day together, sharing a meal, and giving gifts to the children. We had a Christmas tree but no other decorations up. We noted that even George scaled back—he didn't ring the doorbell on Christmas Eve. After the presents were opened, Oscar, age five, and Mahala, age four, came running out of the sunroom, wide-eyed and out of breath. "The light turned off and on! It turned off by itself! It blinked off and then came on!" They were so excited, they were talking over each other. With great precision, they used their hands to demonstrate how long the light was off before it came back on. We discussed the various possibilities and decided that maybe George had stopped by to wish us a Merry Christmas after all, with a new greeting to reflect this year's simpler holiday celebration.

The angel statue in my front yard.

The evening advanced. The shadows lengthened.
The waters of the lake grew pitchy black. The gliding
of the ghostly swans became rare and more rare.
Wilke Collins

❧

Snowy Owl in the Cemetery: Animal Visions and Messengers

I believe that animals and birds and even things in nature, like wind or flowers, can bring messages from the spirit world. Last year, on my birthday, there was a friendly rabbit in my back yard when I left the house, and another one, or maybe the same one, in the yard when I got home at the end of the day. I usually only see one or two rabbits in my yard a month, and I'm very fond of rabbits, so I interpreted the rabbit stopping by as a birthday greeting. That same day, my rose bush, which had bloomed only a few times that summer, had a single, intense pink bloom—very unusual, since my birthday is in the middle of October.

It's been my experience that birds especially bring messages related to spiritual or significant life matters. This makes sense to me, since birds are associated with the element of air that, like the spirit world, is invisible but real. I have found that when I dream about owls, ghost owls in particular, I need to pay attention to the dream's message.

My first owl dream occurred shortly after my husband, John, and I split up. In it, I dreamt that I was in my front yard in Hudson. There were three birds in one of the three tall boulevard elms that were actually in my yard before we lost them to Dutch elm disease in the 1980s.

❧

I was aware in my dream that John and I were no longer together, and that I had the rest of my life ahead of me. The three birds—an owl, a bald eagle, and a tiny bird that was so young it was unidentifiable—represented choices, and I was to decide which one to focus on first, knowing the others would be there when I was ready for them. I figured that the eagle represented freedom, the owl wisdom or education, and the baby bird was an unknown and as yet possibly unformed path. I felt drawn to the owl, and as soon as I chose it in my mind, the owl lifted up off the tree branch and gently flew down to me. I was surprised but stuck my arm out, and the owl landed on it. (I looked up the dream owl later and identified it as a great horned owl.) He felt amazingly heavy, and as I waited to see what would happen next, the owl looked me in the eye—then, still hanging on to my arm, fell forward and hung upside down. That's when I woke up, feeling a buzzy, hypercharged energy that told me the dream was more than a dream. I felt this dream confirmed my decision to stay in college and get my degree even though it would be quite a challenge financially and otherwise. (I was in the middle of my freshman year at the College of St. Catherine when John and I split up.)

The second owl dream I had was that a ghost owl flew in through the big picture window of my house. Once again, the owl paused and looked me right in the eye before it turned and flew down the hall to my bedroom. Even in my dream, a chill went through me when I saw the wisdom and awareness in the owl's eyes. According to Ted Andrews in *Animal Speak*, my favorite book for deciphering animal signs, the ghost owl is "an old symbol of spirit and ghostly contact." And, "It is an owl whose medicine can connect you to old haunts and spirits of properties and homes that may still be lingering about." This dream came at a time when I was undergoing significant changes in my spiritual beliefs, and like the first dream, I woke up with a sense that something important had happened. I believe this dream was a confirmation of the rightness of the spiritual path I was taking.

In the third owl dream, I was back in our house in Hudson, years after we'd moved away. I went down to the laundry room and discovered piles and stacks of dirty clothes everywhere: on the floor, in the sink, on top of the washer and dryer. I started to gather up all the dirty laundry to sort it out, then realized none of it was mine. Even so, I decided to take the wet clothes out of the washing machine and put them in the dryer, at least. When I reached in the washer, I was shocked to discover a ghost owl inside, wet, shivering, and barely alive. I knew I was responsible for the owl, and I picked it up gently and held it against my body, trying to warm it up. I could feel its damp feathers, its bones, and its heart beating rapidly. I also sensed the owl's gratitude at being saved. I carried the shivering bird carefully up the basement steps and walked past a powerful wizard who was sitting at my kitchen table. The wizard nodded his approval, then I stepped outside and opened my arms, and the ghost owl flew away. I believe the message of this dream was that I was trying to take on too much of other people's problems, and doing so was taking a big toll on my soul—and, therefore, my own power.

Another time birds have played a messenger role in my life was when Levi and I first started going out. We had gone on a Sunday drive on some winding, wooded back roads in Wisconsin when I noticed a huge bird's shadow that appeared to be flying on the road in front of us. The shadow was so big that it seemed like it must be an optical illusion. I gasped and pointed. Levi saw it too. Then we looked up and saw a hawk, which Levi told me is one of the birds he most admires. A few minutes later, we stopped by a shallow, clear creek and got out to walk around. We heard some sort of kerfluffle up in the treetops, then saw the shadow of another large bird, this time flying across the water. I only saw its shadow, but Levi spotted the bird and said it was an owl. I said, "That's funny, because owls are my totem bird." We thought the sightings were a good omen for our relationship.

Sometimes, I believe real or spirit realm totem animals make an appearance to offer protection. I used to clean houses for a living while writing freelance stories. Because I only cleaned for families whose vibe

I liked, and I spent many quiet hours in my customers' homes, I became attuned to the energy of their households. Some of my customers were home while I worked, and we'd often have long discussions about everything from family matters to world politics. One of my customers, Lydia, was a homeopathic practitioner, which is a healer who uses natural remedies to spur healing on an energetic level. I had two unusual experiences at Lydia's house. The first was when she had a houseguest, a friend from California, staying with her. Every time her friend came into the room where I was working, I jumped. Once I came around the corner into the family room and nearly walked into him, which also startled me, as usually I am pretty good at tuning in to people. My inability to sense him at all was odd, and I mentioned it to Lydia the next time I cleaned for her after he had gone home. Lydia speculated that perhaps I couldn't tune in to him because his vibe was really refined from practicing meditation on a regular basis for more than twenty-five years.

The other event at Lydia's was more dramatic. One afternoon, while I was alone cleaning, I opened the mud room door to put a mop and bucket in the attached garage. There, in the garage, in the middle of a perfectly ordinary afternoon, I saw a wolf. It was sitting on a riding lawn mower amidst the bikes and rakes and miscellaneous yard stuff. I know it sounds like a funny visual, but the wolf's vibe was actually powerful and dignified. The wolf looked at me calmly, and I got a sense of its serenity and strength. I knew I was seeing a spirit or astral being, because the wolf looked like a photographic negative and was partially transparent. I blinked a few times, but the wolf was still there. I nodded at the wolf, feeling that there was something important about it that needed to be acknowledged. Then I went back in the house, but curiosity got the better of me. Had the wolf been some sort of optical illusion? I opened the door again. The wolf was still in the same place. I got goose bumps on my skin and thanked the universe for the experience of seeing this vision. Then the wolf faded away.

I told Lydia about it when she got back. She was very interested and wanted to know, almost in an urgent way, if there was anything else I could tell her about the experience. She had a number of serious health problems, and she told me that she had been near death a few times in her life. Wolves were her totem animals, and in the past she had seen them when her life was in danger. Once, when she spent weeks in bed recovering from a serious illness, she said she often saw two wolves lying calmly at the foot of her bed, watching her. Lydia was going through a very stressful time in her life when I cleaned for her, but she did not have any health crises in the remaining months that I worked for her. Sadly, I did learn that Lydia died unexpectedly a few years after I had stopped cleaning to start working full-time as a writer. When I think of the many health struggles in Lydia's life, I always envision her totem wolf's strength and peacefulness, and it brings me some consolation.

My great-aunt Norah was a much-loved member of our family, who, along with her husband, Victor, hosted the family Thanksgiving and Easter galas, as well as innumerable other family parties for more than four decades, starting in the 1950s. A week before Norah died, I had a dream in which my friend Anastasia told me she had talked to Grandma Dorrie's spirit, and my grandma had told her that something important was going to happen in one week. I wrote about the experience in my first book. In the dream, Anastasia had seemed positive and peaceful as she relayed the news. One of my main concerns, after waking up, was that something was going to happen to one of my kids. At work the next day, I asked Anastasia for her opinion of the dream. She said to trust the dream's vibe and appreciate my grandma sending a message to me. Norah passed away one week after I had this dream, so I feel it was my grandma letting me know that, as sad as it would be for us to lose Norah, her husband Victor and the Irish relatives would be waiting for her on the other side. Norah was the last of Great-Grandma Maggie's children still living, and it was hard to imagine what our family celebrations would be like with Dorrie, Nellie, and now Norah gone.

On the day of Norah's funeral, my mom, dad, and I received messages from the other side, which we took as signs that Norah was with the rest of the family in spirit and doing fine. Norah passed away in the wintertime, and on our way to the Fort Snelling cemetery where the interment was going to take place, I saw a pure white owl sitting in a bare tree near the cemetery. Molly and I were riding to the cemetery with my parents, and I yelped in surprise and pointed at the owl. I've lived in this area for nearly forty years and, although I know there are owls around, I had never encountered one before. (The owl- and hawk-spotting day with Levi was still in the future at this time.) It was the middle of the day, and the owl was in a tree that was very close to a busy freeway and the Minneapolis/St. Paul international airport. My parents didn't look quickly enough to see the owl, but Molly did. We wondered if it was a sign of some sort. Then my mom told me that on their way to the funeral that morning, she and my dad had seen two beautiful white swans in a cornfield, which was really unusual too. At work the next day, I went online to identify the white owl I had seen and verified that it was a snowy owl. I consulted *Animal Speak* and learned that one of the things owls symbolize is the ability to see things that are hidden and to discover secrets. I felt the white color represented spiritual matters and hope, so the snowy owl seemed like a perfectly fitting omen for the day. I also discovered that swans represent both lasting love and the ability to link different worlds and dimensions, so they, too, served as a powerful message of reassurance.

· · · · · ·

My young cousin Alexandra died last fall. Alexandra and her newborn baby Shea lived with me for a short time about seven years ago, and I wrote about the experience in my first book. At the time she stayed with me, Alexandra was trying to make the difficult decision of whether or not to place Shea for adoption. I felt the Irish family spirits around us, helping out with everything from offering love and support to picking up one of the baby's bottles and putting it in the sink.

There were a lot of signs in the month or so leading up to Alexandra's passing, but I didn't start putting them together until the day before she died. The first unusual thing happened in September, when my mom and I saw an eagle fly up to the picture window at my parents' house while my mom and I were at the dining room table talking. We both remarked on it, because it was so strange to see an eagle come within twenty or twenty-five feet of the house. Usually, the eagles stayed off in the distance, flying over the fields and pine woods.

The next thing to happen was that Molly, who was staying at my house, woke up on my birthday at 5:21 in the morning because she could hear a woman crying and saying, "That's so sad! That's just so sad!" After the initial exclamations, the woman was silent. Molly thought it was me talking on the phone, and she figured someone must have died. Then she realized the house was completely dark and that no one in the house was talking or even awake. After listening for another moment or two, Molly concluded one of the ghosts was back. Molly told me about it the next morning. I asked her if the voice sounded familiar, and she said no. So we figured it was a voice from the past. This was also the day that I saw two rabbits and the bloom on my rose plant, so all in all, I felt that nothing was amiss. In my house, haunting activity tends to escalate in the dark months of the year, generally peaking in October and winding down after Christmas.

In the week before Alexandra's death, I had three experiences with birds that signified something was awry. The first sign was that I noticed a goldfinch watching me from right outside the window. I sometimes see birds in the birdbath or by the feeders for a bit before they fly away, but this was different. This goldfinch was on the sill of the bathroom window, looking in. I was at the sink brushing my teeth when I became aware if it. The bird didn't fly away when I turned to look at it, which sent an odd little ripple through my energy field. This happened on a Saturday.

The second bird event occurred four days later, on Wednesday. A bird got in our back screened porch and was killed by one of the cats. We were very sad when we discovered the bird's body and figured it must have come in through a gap under the door. I've lived in my house for fifteen years, and we've only had one bird get in the porch before (and he flew out when we opened the door).

The third sign happened on the day before Alexandra passed away. I was out decorating the clothesline pole with Indian corn when a goldfinch came flying around the house and almost ran into my forehead. It turned sharply and flew back the way it came. I saw my parents later that day and told them that something was up. My mom and dad and I discussed it briefly but really couldn't come up with an explanation of what the unusual bird behavior meant. I love goldfinches, but in my life they usually signify endings. The next morning, I got the call about Alexandra.

I only made one phone call to let a family member know what had happened, as many people had already been called with the news. When I called my aunt Diana, she said she knew by the sound of my voice that someone had died. (It was Diana's husband Jerry who dreamt of Grandma Dorrie leading someone away shortly before Alexandra passed away.) When I told her it was Alexandra, she gasped and said, "That's so sad! That's just so sad!" As soon as I heard those words, Molly's precognitive experience of waking up and hearing the crying woman came back to me.

At the funeral service, Alexandra's mom and stepdad brought a framed eagle picture to add to the photograph boards. They said that Alexandra had absolutely loved eagles, which I hadn't known. I thought of the eagle that my mom and I had seen fly up to the window a month earlier and wondered if that had been the first sign.

Alexandra, who was fiercely proud of her Irish ancestry and family history, was laid to rest at the same cemetery as our other Irish relatives, on the sunny hillside where Great-Aunt Mimi, Great-Grandma Maggie, and Great-Grandpa Thomas were buried. It was a beautiful, sunny late fall afternoon when we said goodbye to Alexandra, and as I looked out at the rolling hills and blue sky, the familiar Irish blessing came to mind: *May the road rise up to meet you and the wind be always at your back.*

I walked back to my car with Jackie, the wonderful woman who, with her husband, Bill, had adopted Alexandra's daughter Shea seven years earlier. They have created a strong, loving family for Shea and also keep in touch with our family, getting together for a visit once or twice a year. Jackie and I were talking about Alexandra and her life when, seemingly out of nowhere, a little wild breeze kicked up. The breeze was strong enough that I had to grab my hair and hold it in a ponytail to keep it out of my face as I unlocked my car. Jackie asked me what I thought of the sudden wind. I told her I thought it was kind of crazy.

Then she said, "Do you think Alexandra sent it? Like the Irish poem?"

And I laughed and said, "That's *exactly* what I think!" because Alexandra had a definite flair for drama. (When I called Alexandra's mom, Margie, to ask permission to include this story, she said, "Oh, yes! She'd get a kick out of it.") Sending us all on our way with a wild Irish wind was a fitting farewell from Alexandra.

· · · · · ·

MAY THE ROAD rise up to meet you.
May the wind be always at your back.
May the sun shine warm upon your face,
the rains fall soft upon your fields, and until we meet again,
may God hold you in the palm of his hand.
Traditional Gaelic Blessing

My cat Sugar.

Cats come and go without ever leaving.
Martha Curtis

꙰

The Ghost Cat and Mouse Magic: Animal Spirits and Strangeness

Of course, a haunted house wouldn't be complete without a resident ghost cat, and apparently one lives in my house alongside the real cats who spend their days curled up on the radiators and watching birds from the bay window in the kitchen. The ghost cat is white and has been seen by two psychics on different occasions—Robert Baca (who also tuned in to the mentally ill ghost and the ghost girl Sarah) and Maria Shaw, the psychic and astrologer who writes a column for the National Enquirer. Maria, who stopped by for a tour of my house when she was in town, informed me that this house has always been a cat house. I'm inclined to think that the ghost cat lived here at one time, and like many of the people who once lived here, just likes to stop by for visits every now and then.

Two friends of mine who are not psychic, Derrick and Dallas, were actually the first people to see the ghost cat when they spent the night several years ago. Derrick and Dallas not only saw the white ghost cat fighting with my cat Sugar, but they heard it yowling, and it even bit Derrick's toes. The next morning, my friends didn't believe at first that the white cat wasn't real, until we walked around my house and did a tour of cats. Only after they scrutinized all of my cats and ruled them out as the culprit did they accept that the white cat must have been a spirit.

I've had many unusual experiences with real animals throughout my life, like when our cat Patches had a kitten in my lap. I was in fifth grade, and my brothers and sisters and I were watching TV. Except for the flickering light from the television, it was dark in the living room. I was on the floor holding Patches when I felt something warm and sticky on my leg. I yelled, and someone turned on the light. A tiny newborn kitten was wriggling around on my thigh. We got a cardboard box for Patches to use as a delivery room while giving birth to the rest of her kittens, but I always felt special that Patches trusted me that much.

When we lived in Ottawa, a neighbor's Shetland pony kept running away from her owner and coming to our house. My dad finally just bought the horse for ten dollars, and we named her Old Paint because of her coloring. My most vivid memory of Old Paint is going out to the pasture to pet her and her pulling off my cap and trying to eat my hair.

When we lived South Dakota, a mountain goat wandered into our yard, and a family of spray-happy skunks moved into the crawl space under our house. An abused dog that was part German shepherd and part wolf also made her way to our house. We already had our boxers Duke and Duchess, but we kept the wolf dog, too. My mom named her Lobo, which is a play on *loup*, the French word for wolf. Lobo was very loving to everyone in our family but usually bit anyone else who came on our property.

In Hudson, Wisconsin, living right in town, my kids and I tried to catch a young runaway pig in our neighborhood, a broken-off piece of twine still tied around her neck. Here in Sibley, also right in town, I discovered a black sheep in my back yard one afternoon. It turns out the sheep was an escapee from a pageant of some sort. And we had a three-legged bunny in our neighborhood for one entire summer. The rabbit was notorious for her unusual boldness. I'd see her lounging all stretched out by my birdbath or calmly munching clover out in the open yard in the middle of the day. I liked the three-legged bunny but my neighbor Tabitha did not. She said the rabbit stared at her in an odd way.

When my beau Levi and I first met, he commented on how my refrigerator magnet of a friendly yellow lab mutt looked exactly like a dog someone had given him in the 1970s.

"My mom gave me that magnet because it looks just like a dog someone gave *me* in the seventies!" I told him.

In talking further, we discovered another coincidence—both of our dogs had been killed by wild animals in northern Minnesota. My dog, Sandy, was killed by a bear while saving someone's life. Her new owner, a truck driver friend of my dad's, told me Sandy had saved his life by alerting him to the bear's presence in his yard and fighting the bear while he ran for his gun. Levi's dog, Floep (named by Dutch friends he had met while living in Africa), was killed by a pack of timber wolves.

During the 1980s and '90s, my mom's dog George would come to stay at my house every now and then, while my parents were traveling. George didn't like spending time with my cats, and he didn't like the way his toenails clicked on our hardwood floors. But most of all, George didn't like being away from my mom, whom he adored. Still, in his quiet, worried way, George was a trooper.

George was a Jack Russell terrier mix. We thought of George as a small dog, since my parents usually had big dogs like boxers, labradors, and, of course, Lobo, who was part wolf. But as far as Jack Russell terriers go, George was big. At the time, pot-bellied pigs were popular, and George reminded me of one, with his short legs, stout body, and black and white coloring. But when I made that observation to a truck driver friend named Bud Shekalowski, who was at my house replacing the old two-prong outlets with new grounded ones, he told me George didn't appreciate the comparison. Bud had been struck by lightning once and electrocuted another time and told me that ever since, he had been able to read minds. He also told me George had some sort of problem with his left eye. I apologized to George for saying he resembled a pot-bellied pig and mentioned to him how smart pigs are. When my parents came to pick up George, I told my mom what Bud had told me. A week later, my mom called to tell me that she'd had to bring George to the vet because his left eye was red and sore. Hearing what George was thinking made me curious about what my cats might say if they could talk. (At the time, Theo and Sugar, along with Jack's cat, Boo, were living at my house.) It also made me wonder if I could check in with the spirit of our dog Rascal, whose parents were Lobo and Duke. I did some searching and found an animal psychic named Mary Stoffel. I tried to get my then-beau Rex to ask Mary about some animal in his life, but he said since he didn't have any companion animals, he'd have to ask about the spiders in his basement, and he didn't care what they thought.

When I called, the first thing Mary said to me was, "Your house is filled with spirits. Are you okay with that?" This was before my book came out, and Mary had no idea who I was or where I lived. I told her I was okay with it, and we continued on with the reading. I asked Mary if she could connect with animals in the spirit world. I wanted to get in touch with Rascal. Rascal had died nearly twenty years earlier. Mary said she had never gone back that far in time, but she would give it a try. She asked me for his name, and then she tuned in. "Is Rascal a big dog, rangy, with strong masculine energy?" she asked.

"Yes," I said.

"Hmm …" Mary paused for a minute. "I'm not sure this is your dog. This being has a touch of the wild in him, like he's not completely a domesticated animal."

"No, that's Rascal!" I said. "His mother was part wolf." Mary then told me that one of Rascal's chosen tasks for his lifetime was to learn how to live peacefully with humans. She said he was doing fine and was glad he had spent time with our family.

With that bit of communication taken care of, we moved on to the fun of hearing what the three cats had to say. Mary was so taken with Theo's peaceful and wise vibe that she said she just wanted to soak it in for a moment. Theo told her when we moved into this house, he didn't know if he could deal with all the ghosts and astral stuff going on. Mary told me that Theo not only learned to deal with it, but he was acting as sort of a sentry for the astral realm of the house. She said that he would let me know when weird stuff was going on. I thought of how when we first moved in, Theo had started to display the really odd behavior of standing on his hind legs for no apparent reason. It was very disconcerting to walk into a room and see a cat standing in the middle of it. Mary said Theo was like a familiar for me, in that he was a partner in keeping our home's vibe clear and positive.

Mary next tuned in to Sugar Plum. She said that while Theo watched over the astral realm of our house, Sugar was in charge of the physical realm. Sugar told Mary that we had people coming and going all the time, which was true. Between kids, family parties, friends, and foster care clients at my house one or two weekends a month, our household was usually bustling. Mary said Sugar was like a social ambassador—she greeted visitors and was the most outgoing of our cats, which was true. My favorite Sugar quote was when she told Mary, "I've got my paws full taking care of all the people that she has coming and going."

Boo was last, and Mary said Boo wanted a clearly defined role in the household since Sugar and Theo were both doing important tasks. Mary said Boo was a natural hunter and wanted to hunt something. Mary asked if we had any mice in the house that Boo could take care of for us. I like the idea of cats scaring mice away rather than killing them, but at the time, we had never seen a mouse in our house. I was really impressed that Mary had tuned in to each cat's vibe so well. We had gotten Boo from our neighbor, and I knew that Boo's dad hunted bunnies and her mom was a bird killer.

After the experience with Mary, I tried to use animal communication techniques on some hornets that had built a mean-looking paper nest on my front porch. It was the first time there had ever been a hive on my house, and the hive was on a corner of the house near the Catholic school. This was during the time when a highly charged debate was going on about the school putting up temporary classrooms in their parking lot. The hive was on the corner of my house that pointed right at the school, and I wondered if it represented all the buzzy emotions swirling around the issue. For all my fears of spiders and other creepy-crawly things, I am weirdly unafraid of bees, wasps, and hornets. I decided to try to connect with the hornets. I stood on the sidewalk and tried to tune in. I sent out the message that my front porch wasn't an ideal location for their nest from my perspective, but I was going to leave their home alone until they were done with it in the fall, then take it down. The response I got was a disdainful "Pfffft"—like, "No kidding, you're going to leave it alone." And although I don't know whether or not that was what the hornets were actually thinking, their hornet friends did not show up to build a hive on my porch the next year.

One of my favorite Sugar Plum stories happened when a film crew was at my house one night. One of the guests was a woman who did automatic writing, which meant she acted as a channel, sitting with a pen and notebook, letting spirits express themselves through her. (The late author Ruth Montgomery wrote several best-selling metaphysical books via automatic writing using her typewriter.) The channel was filmed in the playroom, which is sunny and cheerful in the daytime but at night gets an ominous vibe that is commented on by nearly everyone who comes through my house. (This is the room that we no longer use as a bedroom because of some of the scary haunting things that have happened in it.)

The channel was sitting on the floor with a pen and a notebook in her hand. There was a camera person in the room with her, but most of us were in a different part of the house with Robert Baca and the other camera person. The cameras were rolling, but the spirits weren't cooperating. Sugar, who loves to be part of whatever is going on, watched with interest. After a few minutes of nothing happening, Sugar apparently decided to take matters into her own paws. She jumped into the channel's lap, put her paw on the pen, and dragged the pen across the page. We weren't able to decipher Sugar's scribble—I guess she just wanted to add some drama to the film shoot—but I still have Sugie's "automatic writing" in a drawer.

The spirits of both David Grey Hair and Theo, our much-loved family cats, have also visited. Both cats lived to be nearly twenty years old and were the source of a lot of happiness in our family. Both David and Theo were with us while my kids Molly and Jack were growing up, which made their passing even more difficult, as they were a tie to one of the most satisfying and meaningful periods in my life. I wrote about David's visit in my first book. I woke up one night a few years after he died and saw him, healthy and fine, sitting outside my bedroom window on the roof of the back porch. I was having an out-of-body experience at the time, and as happy as I was to see David, I really wanted to touch him and hold him, too. I realized that in an astral state, I should be able to reach through the window glass. I gave it a try. The glass felt heavy and draggy, but my hands and arms went through the window. I was able to pet David again and tell him how much he meant to us and how much we missed him.

Theo died two years ago. He was eighteen and a half, and his thyroid went crazy. He also had kidney problems. We tried to humanely treat both conditions and keep him comfortable, but his last few months were pretty grim. I believe that if a cat is no longer able to eat, is in extreme pain, or seems not to want to live any longer, it's time to put him or her down. Otherwise, they get whatever care they need for as long as they need it.

One night shortly before Theo died, he could no longer climb the stairs. He slept in a corner of the living room, and I slept on the couch so I could be near him. The next morning when I woke up, I started to cry when I saw my beautiful Theo, scrawny and weak, still in the exact same spot he had been the night before. Theo looked at me, then came over to the couch. He jumped up on the couch—I don't know how—and put his paw on my cheek. He looked directly into my eyes. He remained this way for almost a minute. I told him we loved him and thanked him for all the things we had learned from him. I told him to let me know when he was ready to go.

A few days after this happened, I came home from work and it was evident that Theo was dying. I called our vet and asked if it would be more humane to let Theo die naturally or to put him down. The vet, Dr. Filkins, said it could take Theo a day or more to die, and it would be better to put him down. When he got the call to come to my house, Dr. Filkins was out for ice cream with his wife, so they came together. The people at our vet's office have provided care for our cats for fifteen years, and we consider all of them friends. I called Molly and Jack, and they came over. We said our goodbyes to Theo. It was summertime, and when Dr. Filkins arrived, we brought Theo out to the flower garden under the angel statue. Dr. Filkins gave Theo the shot and, in an instant, Theo was gone.

I had read in a Diane Stein book that, if possible, you should stay with your companion animal's body for three hours after they die, as it takes that long for their spirit to completely disengage from their physical body. We had Theo on a soft blanket. We brushed Theo's fur, which had gotten matted and dull during his illness. (He'd been too frail and sore during his last few months to tolerate being groomed.) We put flowers and sweet-smelling blooms from the trees across the street on his body. It was very comforting to spend some time with Theo and be part of taking care of his body one last time. It makes me think we have really lost an important ritual with our modern-day funeral and burial practices. My kids and I talked about all the ways Theo had made our lives more interesting and enjoyable. We brought Sugar over to say goodbye to Theo, but she didn't even seem to realize his body was there. After an hour or so, we put Theo's body, wrapped in the towel, into a clear plastic container with the lid off. He looked like he was sleeping. We left him on the back porch, and the next morning, I said goodbye and petted his head one last time before bringing him to the vet to be cremated. It took a few weeks to get Theo's ashes back, and I was still having a hard time dealing with him being gone. I put off burying his ashes for a few months, and in the meantime, Molly had moved to Savannah, Georgia, to go to grad school. I finally decided on a beautiful September day that

I should take care of his ashes while the weather was still good. Jack was in London on a business trip, so I just did a small ceremony myself, burying Theo's ashes in the same flower garden where the ashes of our cat David and Itty, Molly's pygmy hedgehog, are buried. It was difficult, but I felt much better afterward. The next day, Molly called me from Savannah. "Did you finally bury Theo's ashes yesterday?" she asked.

"Yes," I said. I hadn't told either of the kids about the ceremony, since I had decided to do it on the spur of the moment.

"I knew it! Theo came to me in a dream last night, Mom," Molly said. "He looked healthy and happy, and he kissed me on the nose. I think he wanted to let us know that he is fine."

Theo's spirit visited our house on one other occasion. Since my book came out, I have started offering haunted tea parties in order to accommodate all the requests I get from people to see my home. A Girl Scout leader named Amanda sent me an email to see if she could schedule a haunted tea party for her troop. She was going to stop by to pick up my book to read before the party. It was a beautiful fall day, a little more than a year after Theo died. The boulevard maples were starting to turn orange and yellow, and the sky was bright with the blue sunshine of September.

While waiting for Amanda to stop by, I was upstairs in my bedroom. My cats Sugar and Fluffy (both of whom got their fabulous names from young girls) were in the room with me. I was petting the cats, watching the curtains blow gently in the breeze. I wished Theo could be with us to enjoy the perfect shimmering vibe of the day. It was the first time since the burial ceremony that I had really thought about how much I missed him. Suddenly, I felt Theo's presence. I looked around hopefully. I asked Theo to let me know if he was with us. I waited a few minutes but didn't see him. I still felt he was with us, enjoying a shared moment on a perfect autumn afternoon, so I told Theo we loved him and missed him and hoped he was well.

Amanda and her daughter Mia arrived a few minutes later. They were so nice that I invited them in for a quick tour while we discussed the logistics of the Girl Scout tea party. While standing in the back hall-way of the house, Mia suddenly fell backwards, as though she had been pushed. "What just happened?" I asked.

Mia said, "I don't know—suddenly, I just fell over!"

I realized that Mia had been standing right in one of the main portals in our house, the doorway between the back hall and summer kitchen. So much weird stuff has happened in the back hallway that our friend Sonya gave us a "ghost crossing" sign to hang on the wall along with the framed house blessing and vintage holy water dispenser that were already there. My friend Cowgirl Josie saw Leon back there one night, peering around the corner, as we finished up the final preparations for a party. Other guests have felt the skin-prickly, supercharged atmosphere that sometimes pervades the area or even felt something brush against them. On two separate occasions, our guests' cell phones have acted strange in the vicinity of the portal. One phone rang when it was turned off (and continued to misbehave on the way home). Another phone delivered two phantom calls and a text message from nowhere that even the phone company couldn't explain. I was just about to mention the portal when Amanda gasped and pointed into the hallway behind Mia.

"What?" Mia and I both said at once.

"I just saw a cat, and it disappeared right in front of my eyes!" Amanda said.

"Well, we do have a ghost cat here," I said. "Was it white?"

"No, it was black with a white bib. It came out from behind that hall door and disappeared."

Now it was my turn to catch my breath. Theo! He had shown up after all. He was black with a white bib, and one of his favorite hiding spots was behind the hall door. I got choked up, and so did Amanda and Mia when they heard the story of me talking to Theo just before they came. Amanda was especially excited by the experience because she had never seen a spirit before.

My very favorite weird animal experience was the mouse miracle. I was watching TV one night with my beau at the time, Rex, and he saw something race across the kitchen floor. At the time, Theo, Sugar, and Jack's cat Boo were living at home. The cats all ran into the parlor. We followed them and saw they had chased a mouse under the piano. I put the cats in the other room while Rex got a broom. I had the idea that I would grab the mouse by the tail and bring it safely out the front door. Rex seemed a little skeptical of this plan, but I had occasionally held my kids' pet gerbil years before, so I felt like I actually might be able to touch a mouse long enough to get him out the door. What I really wanted was for the mouse to go to the front door, and I could just open the door and let him out. That is the picture I had in my mind—and that is exactly what happened the next night.

We couldn't scare the mouse out from under the piano and we didn't want to move the piano and squish him either. I didn't want to set a trap, and I didn't want the mouse to die at the paws of my cats. I closed the parlor doors, and Rex and I went to bed.

The next morning, I opened up the parlor, hoping the mouse might have somehow escaped outside during the night. When all three cats ran straight to the radiator, I surmised the mouse was still in the room. I shooed the cats out. I figured the mouse was probably exhausted and hungry, so I did Reiki to protect the mouse. I tried to communicate with him to encourage him to leave my house the way he came, but I didn't feel like I connected with him. The impression I got was that the mouse's consciousness was too small and his stress too great to connect with him in any meaningful way. Then I got the idea that I needed to communicate with something bigger than the mouse, like a guardian or oversoul of mice. So I sent the message out to whoever is in charge of mice to try to encourage this mouse to leave the house the way he came in. I went to work feeling very sorry for the mouse.

When I got home that night, I gingerly made my way through the house, afraid I would encounter the gory aftermath of a cat and mouse game. I breathed easier when I realized the mouse was either outside or in a new hiding spot. I let the cats out on the back screened porch and worked in the yard until dark. When I came in the house at 10 PM,

I felt grounded and happy, the way I usually do after spending time in my yard. I turned on the front hall light as I headed upstairs, and there, sitting on his haunches a foot away from the front door, was the little mouse! I thanked the mouse guardian or whoever brought him there. When he saw me, the mouse ran and hid behind a vase of flowers at the base of the coat rack, but he kept watching to see what was happening. (I could see him because there is a full-length mirror on the coat rack.) I ran to the kitchen to get a broom, just in case he ran toward my legs, which were bare. I asked the mouse guardian to guide the mouse toward freedom as I slowly opened the front door. Then I opened the screen door as wide as I could and propped it open with the slider thing on the top. I was just starting to wonder how I was going to coax the mouse around the interior door (which opened inward and would have made it necessary for the mouse to make a wide arc back in towards the interior of the house). But the mouse figured out the most direct escape route before I did. He raced forward, through the inch-or-so clearance between the doorframe and the door, and ran out the door at full speed before dropping out of sight off the edge of the porch. I called Rex and said, "I have just witnessed a mouse miracle. The little mouse has left the building, and he went out through the front door."

· · · · · ·

This chapter took a week to write. I had a hard time finishing it for some reason, maybe because I was writing about saying goodbye to Theo. I finally decided that maybe I should set it aside and go on to a different chapter, even though I like to finish one chapter before starting another. I was still debating the matter when I got home from working out with Molly and Jack. As I walked through the front hall, I turned on the front porch light. There, sitting right at the front door, was a big white cat with a heavy winter coat. I had never seen this cat before around the neighborhood. The white cat got up and strode around the porch for a while, then walked down the porch steps and then the front walk, down another set of steps, and finally to the end of my carriage sidewalk.

I took this white cat as a sign from the universe that everything was going to be fine. I was going to start this chapter with a ghost cat and end it with a mouse miracle, but I guess instead the chapter starts and ends with white cats, one a ghost and the other a messenger.

Fish-scale pattern similar to that on ceremonial
robe worn by Asian spirit in doorway (this image
is from Dover's Japanese Stencil Designs).

It is far harder to kill a phantom than a reality.
Virginia Woolf

❧❧

The Ghost Eater
and Other Stories from
the Magical Bookstore

After *House of Spirits and Whispers* came out, one of my first
author events was at Magus Books in Minneapolis. A popular and well-respected bookstore, Magus is frequented by college stu-
dents from the nearby University of Minnesota campus as well as witches, wizards, herbalists, and magical people of all sorts. Because I'm such
a terrible driver in the city, I had never been to Magus, even though
I'd heard people rave about it for years. I was excited about making an
appearance there and looked forward to meeting the fabled Roger, the
Englishman who had started Magus Books fifteen years earlier. I didn't
know exactly what to expect, but I figured it would be an interesting
experience. I brought along pictures of some of the spirits in my house,
a homemade coffee-can safe that Leon, the former owner and main
house spirit, had hidden in the basement dirt room, and a bottle of wine
for Roger. By the end of the night, I had heard some of the most disturbing ghost stories I'd ever heard in my life, learned some new things
about astral beings, and been followed home by a new ghost. I also sold
a few books.

This author appearance was one of the few times I brought along a small entourage of friends. It was a good thing I did, as only four other people showed up—a young married couple, a man who hardly spoke but took copious notes, and a paranormal investigator. In retrospect, I attribute the small turnout to the probability that true haunted house stories are no big deal to people who work with spirits and cast spells on a regular basis. I had invited my former beau Rex, my friend and publicist Kelly, and my friend and fellow writer Carmine, who gave me a lift to the bookstore so I wouldn't have to drive. Given the size of the group, I decided the best approach would be to set up a storytelling circle in the back corner where the book signing was going to take place. I had filled Leon's homemade coffee-can safe with Tootsie Rolls and lollipops, passed it around with the spirit pictures, and started telling the story of my house. A few shoppers meandered around the store, and Roger listened from behind the checkout counter.

The young couple said they were interested in haunted houses because the wife, Ellen, had lived in a very haunted house in Minneapolis—perhaps dangerously so, as at least one or two renters that lived there before her family moved in had died in the house. Ellen's mom was pregnant with her when they moved into the old Victorian home. Ellen believed that her own psychic abilities were sharpened in response to living in this threatening, haunted environment, as a coping mechanism or possibly even a survival skill. Lori Bogren, from the Minnesota Paranormal Investigators Group, agreed, saying that one of their members was taking a break from investigating because she was pregnant and didn't want to expose her unborn child to any negative entities.

Ellen said the most frightening thing her family experienced was seeing menacing faces appear in the walls and on the TV screen, and that her parents had taken a photograph of one of the faces. Her mom and dad's relationship deteriorated after moving into the house, and they began to fight all the time. Eventually, Ellen's parents split up, and they moved out of the house when she was around four years old.

Someone in the circle asked Ellen if the house was still haunted. She told us that the next renter after them, a man in his thirties or forties, lived in the house for less than a year before he was found dead inside it. She said that her family lost track of who lived in the house after that.

This sobering story actually stopped conversation while we let the idea of a killer house sink in. Then the quiet man picked up his notebook and pen. "What's the address?"

Someone said, "So you never move there?" We all laughed.

As for myself, I had such an acute sense of dread while Ellen was telling her story that I said a protection prayer for all of us. I didn't want any energetic connection to the old house. Even hearing the story made me feel at risk, like whatever was haunting the place might tune in to my awareness and fear, and become aware of me. I would never think of driving past the place to get a closer look. I was impressed when, after the reading, Lori matter-of-factly exchanged contact information with Ellen so Ellen could call if she ever needed help.

People are always asking me how I can live in a haunted house. I have had some very frightening experiences while living in my house, including waking up one night and seeing a dark man who glistened with an oily sheen standing beside my bed, watching me. Another time, I was pinned down in bed by something I couldn't see. When whatever it was finally released me, I sat up in bed and swung my elbow backwards as hard as I could in case the entity was still around. Sitting up and wide awake, I felt it stick its tongue in my ear. For the most part, though, the spirit activity in my house is simply interesting and even companionable, rather than threatening.

Another question I get asked all the time is whether or not I think spirits can hurt people. My answer had always been that I thought it was possible but extremely rare. Now, I wondered if I had been wrong. Ellen's story rattled my sense of security. Was there such a thing as a killer house? In the 1970s, my sisters and I had been so scared by the book *The Amityville Horror* that for a while after reading it, we were too afraid even to go to the bathroom alone. I know questions have been raised about the accuracy of the Amityville story, but Ellen seemed down-to-earth and sincere.

Ellen also told us about being visited by the spirit of an ex-boyfriend who had committed suicide by jumping into the Mississippi River. She was respectful but matter-of-fact when she said that sometimes he had the distorted appearance of someone who had drowned and other times he looked like a Picasso painting, as if she were seeing more planes, or aspects, of him than is normally possible. I found this last detail very interesting, as I have seen a similar effect in some of my astral visions. Sometimes whatever I'm seeing has a Picasso-esque sense of proportion and spatial relationships. I call it the unfolded version of things because it reminds me of the 1970s-era math problems that presented some weird unfolded shape with the impossible to answer question, "What would this look like if it were put back together?" The only other reference I've heard or seen to this "unfolded" state was, once again, in the Peter Tompkins book *The Secret Life of Nature*. When Tompkins tells about the four-dimensional nature of astral vision (the type of vision the Theosophists referred to as "withinth"), Tompkins describes "a sort of four-dimensional sense of seeing an object from all sides at once and from inside as well." He goes on to paraphrase well-known Theosophist Charles Leadbeater, using the example that if you had a cube of wood with writing on all sides, "viewed astrally, all the sides would be visible at once, right way up, as if the cube were flattened."

Lori told us that if a spirit is earthbound and has not yet crossed over, he or she will appear as they did at death. The spirit will be the same age and in the same physical condition, and that's why Ellen saw her former boyfriend in a way that reflected the manner of his death. Lori said the Picasso-type appearance might mean that he perceived himself as stuck in the wrong dimension. Once spirits have crossed over, they realize they can change their appearance to reflect the best or happiest time of their life, or the one most relevant to the person they're visiting. Lori suggested that Ellen encourage her ex-boyfriend to move on and let him know there was nothing to fear.

I thought about seeing Leon's spirit after we found the money and gave it back to his family. He had looked and walked like an old man, as if he had aches and pains and heaviness. The night I saw him, Leon had been in the spirit world for less than a year, and I believe he was still earthbound at the time because he was so concerned about the stuff he had hidden in the basement dirt room. When I saw the old-fashioned spirit sisters in my house, they had been spirits much longer than Leon had, and they looked like traditional ghosts—they were transparent and completely white, and they were floating in the air.

I asked Lori if the bookstore was haunted. She said that because of the magical work people were involved in, there were spirits and entities checking out the bookstore all the time, but that the store employees, who were highly skilled magicians and energy workers themselves, performed cleansing and protective work on a regular basis.

Then Lori, who is clairvoyant, told us about being part of an investigation in which a woman's spirit was being abused by the spirit of the person who had murdered her in the physical world. One of the paranormal investigators and her spirit guide had created a protective space around the woman's spirit, barring the abuser's access to her, while the other investigators focused on persuading her to go to the light. The abusive spirit stood nearby and made threats. Lori could see all the astral beings, and everything seemed to be going smoothly, so she stood back to watch. The abusive spirit kept trying to get to the vulnerable spirit but couldn't. Suddenly, a new entity appeared behind the abusive spirit. Lori said that some would consider the entity a demon, but in her opinion, it was just a form of energy that survived by consuming negative energy. The entity looked at Lori, then ate the abusive spirit and disappeared. And the woman's spirit was able to cross over to the other side.

This story absolutely freaked me out. I believe that Lori was telling the truth about what she saw and perceived, and I was happy that the gentle spirit got free and made it to the light. But I couldn't get my mind around the idea of any entity being allowed to destroy another's soul. It defied my beliefs about the laws of the universe. I believe that there is a divine creative source in the universe, and I also believe that even this divine creator would never vanquish someone's soul. But I listened to Lori's experience and decided I would give the entire matter some more thought. Lori herself took what she had seen that night in stride, as simply a form of survival and, in this case, justice.

Later, I told my friend Ted Hughes about the ghost-eater story to get his opinion on it. Ted is extremely psychic, almost more at home in the astral world than the physical one. He lives in northern California on Mount Shasta, a magnificent place with such a strong spiritual vibe that it's reputed to be the magical home to everything from Lemurians to leprechauns. Many of the area residents are involved in energy healing, magical work, shamanic practices, and earth-centered spirituality. Ted's reasoned response to the ghost-eater story was that there is a place for every being in the universe. He said spirits and other astral beings usually only make trouble when they are stuck in the wrong place. Ted told me about one of his friends who was doing shamanistic healing work for people with harmful energetic attachments in their auras. Ted's friend would remove the offending energy form and send it to be cleansed by the energy of the sun. The friend called Ted when he himself was beset by astral beings wreaking havoc on his aura and health, to the point where black oily stuff was oozing out of the bottoms of his feet. The man had gone to different doctors to get treatment, but none of them had been able to help him.

Ted journeyed to gain insight on the situation and discovered that the astral beings were angry with his friend. Ted explained it to me by saying, "How would you feel if someone sent you or your friends to the sun to be burnt to a crisp?" Ted told his healer friend to change the energy-clearing process he used. Instead of sending unwelcome astral beings to the sun, Ted and his friend started working with the beings so they could go back home. They asked for a gateway to be opened to receive the beings back where they belonged. For those beings that didn't want to go home, they requested that they go to an energetically compatible place where they could be safe and also not harm other beings. Ted said it was kind of like a swap, helping everyone get back to where they belonged. Within a few weeks, Ted's friend was feeling better. Hearing Ted's far-out stories of the astral world, tempered with his low-key positivity and problem-solving approach to things, is one of the things I enjoy most about our friendship.

I was a little wired when I got home the night of the book signing, and I went to bed with a sense of anticipation. I had the feeling something was going to happen. I had been super freaked out by the killer house and ghost-eater stories, but Roger's vibe was so positive and strong that I believed if anything did happen as a result of my visit to the bookstore, it would be all right. I went to bed but woke up an hour and a half later and saw a spirit standing in the doorway of my room. It was a young Asian man, whom I sensed was Japanese. He was wearing a ceremonial black and silver silk gown that had a pattern on it that looked like stylized fish scales. He felt familiar and friendly, even though I had no idea who he might be.

The spirit smiled in a friendly way. In a calm voice, he said, "You must remember, things are not always as they appear." Then he disappeared.

I had a "singing skin" feeling after this experience, which is how I describe the super-charged, buzzy way I feel after a positive spirit encounter. It's a physical kind of hypersensitivity I get when something really moves my soul, like hearing a chillingly beautiful piece of music on Christmas Eve or standing at the top of Machu Pic-chu in Peru with Levi smiling beside me.

I have not been able to come up with any solid explanation for see-ing a spirit from an era and culture so different from my own stand-ing in the doorway of my room. I did ask Roger later if the spirit was connected to him personally, but he said no. Yet, it seems logical to me that the spirit was somehow connected with the bookstore, since I only saw that spirit one time, and it was the night I had been at the bookstore. One possibility I've considered is that the Asian spirit was a guardian of the bookstore. Or, he might even have been a guardian of one of the books at Magus. (One used-bookstore owner I know believes that books possess some form of sentience, a concept I had never considered before but find really intriguing. And intuitive coach Jodi Livon, who conducted a very helpful psychic reading for me recently, told me she usually can't read ghost stories because she can feel the actual spirits coming through when she does. With my book House of Spirits and Whispers, she said she mostly tuned in to my energy, which she found "positive and strong," although she did have to put down my book a few times.) Magus does sell ceremonial weap-ons at the store, including a Kunai wooden athame, which is a replica of an ancient Japanese tool and weapon, so it's possible the spirit was associated with that. Generally speaking, though, it's used or antique items that are most likely to have energy or spirits attached to them.

Maybe the spirit's smiling message was in regard to the ghost eater. That's my best guess for now, since my overriding question that night was whether or not any being could truly destroy another's soul. Per-haps the Asian spirit's cryptic message meant that the ghost eater only appeared to consume the abusive spirit, when in reality he was just removing him from a situation where he didn't belong.

POSTSCRIPT TO THIS STORY: When I contacted Lori Bogren from the paranormal group to get permission to use her name in my book, she clarified for me that, while the entity did appear to devour the abusive spirit, she has the same basic philosophy as my friend Ted. She believes "when it comes to the spirit world, no energy being can destroy the energy of another. They can capture it, hold it in check, send it or force it to go somewhere … at most (the critter that ate the spirit) would imprison it until the critter released it by choice or until something else came along and released it."

Hallway at the Trempealeau Hotel,
Trempealeau, Wisconsin, 2008.

Through the long corridors the ghosts of the
past walk unforbidden, hindered only by broken
promises, dead hopes, and dream-dust.
Myrtle Reed, "Old Rose and Silver"

❧

Room 5 at
the Trempealeau Hotel

This past March, my beau Levi and I decided to celebrate his
birthday by taking a road trip along the Mississippi River. We
headed south from Sibley on the Great River Road with the idea of eventually ending up in La Crosse, Wisconsin. Unlike me and my control-
freak tendencies, Levi is an adventurer who likes to keep things loose
and open to possibility. That's why, after moseying along for several
hours, stopping to eat, walking around the bluff-top roadside parks, and
enjoying the earthy smell of spring in the damp gray breeze, we ended
up with no place to stay for the night. Levi had done a little research
before we embarked on our trip—he'd found three or four different, rustic B & B possibilities along our route, including our first choice, a cabin
that had a tree growing in the living room. We didn't worry about making reservations because it was so early in the season we didn't think
there'd be much demand for rooms. In a way, we were right. It *was* so
early in the season that, at 4 PM or so, when at last we started calling
around to book a room, we found out that none of the B & B's on our list
were even open for business until April.

We decided to keep driving, with the idea that something interesting
would turn up. The highway passed through the picturesque historic

town of Trempealeau, Wisconsin, where an inviting waterfront park with a big clock, old-fashioned street lamps, and a railroad track caught my eye. We drove down for a closer look around, and that's how we discovered the Trempealeau Hotel. Built in the 1880s, the historic hotel is a two-story building with a screened porch, clapboard siding, and a big side yard for concerts and picnics. Levi went in to see if they had any rooms, while I tidied up the car. He came out with a big grin on his face.

"What, what?" I asked.

"You're going to like this hotel." That was all he would say.

We went inside, and I did genuinely appreciate the hotel's character and authenticity. It was a historic building, nice without being fancy, with a few charming antiques and a vintage bar. A door in the main bar room opened to a staircase that led to the hotel section of the property. The bartender told us we could go upstairs and choose any room we liked. She mentioned that no one else would be staying at the hotel that night.

As soon as we started to climb the steep wooden staircase, I knew the place was haunted. Levi said he felt it, too. For all his practical outdoorsman ways, Levi has a hippie soul and an open-minded curiosity about metaphysical matters. Levi felt that the spirit was a woman and that she was watching us as we entered her territory. At the top of the staircase was a small sitting area with a couple of chairs, including an imposing wooden chair with Masonic ceremonial-type carvings and trim, such as a stylized star and globes on the top rail. There was one bathroom upstairs for all the guests to share, European style. An old wooden armoire in the sitting room was filled with books, board games, and puzzles, and there was a basket that held prints of vintage photographs, images of people long since dead. We decided to purchase a photograph of people at the local train depot in the late 1800s, and brought it with us as we made our way down the hallway. Old pictures also lined the walls of the long hallway of doors. I wondered if any of the people in the photographs had been associated with the hotel and if the photographs provided them with an energetic link to the property.

Levi and I stuck our heads in the doorway of every room as we walked past. Each had its own vibe and décor, a wonderful hodgepodge of individuality with old-fashioned iron beds, colorful quilts, and antique dressers or bureaus. Just getting to look into each room and choose the one that suited us was a pleasure. One of the middle rooms had a bit of jangled energy that made me think it might be haunted. The last room, at the end of the hall, was room 5. It was a corner room with two lace-curtained windows, one of which faced the river, and a pretty blue quilt on the bed. Levi and I both felt that the ghost woman hung out in this room, but we loved it and decided it was the room we wanted.

When we went downstairs to pay for our room, we asked the bartender if the hotel was haunted. She smiled and said that some people thought so, but she didn't volunteer any more information. Levi asked the bartender if there was a female ghost upstairs. The bartender said that she hadn't experienced anything herself, but people said the hotel was haunted by the spirit of a woman. The story was that the ghost hung out in room 5, and when people slept in her room, the ghost wandered up and down the hallway and rattled doorknobs, trying to find a place to sleep.

Levi and I looked at each other. "We knew room 5 was haunted!" we told her.

"Which room would you like?" she asked.

We both grinned. "Room 5."

The bartender laughed and shook her head. "That's the room people always choose."

We checked in, then went to dinner at a supper club just a little upriver from the hotel. The supper club was on the road that led to Perrot State Park, which we made plans to visit the next day. When we got back to the hotel, Levi and I had a drink at the bar, then went up to our room. It felt kind of weird to go upstairs to bed while a bar full of people socialized on the main floor, but we couldn't hear any bar noise once we left the room, and no one paid any attention to us at all. The bartender had told us to leave our key on the dresser in the morning, as there would be no one at the hotel after the bar closed. The idea of being the only guests in a haunted hotel felt a little Norman Bates-y. It definitely heightened our anticipation of the night ahead. We decided to put my favorite faux fur hat on the bed of the other room that seemed haunted, as sort of a peace offering and sort of an invitation to the spirit to spend the night in that room instead of her usual hangout. We told the spirit we were happy to be staying at the hotel and invited her to stay in the room with us if she was friendly and quiet. Back in room 5, we lay in bed for a while and listened, but nothing happened and we eventually fell asleep.

At some point in the early morning hours, I woke up. The room was dark. I held my breath and listened. Someone was rattling the door. This was one of the few times in my life where my first thought was that it was an intruder rather than a ghost. "Levi," I whispered. The door rattled again. "Did you hear that?"

"Yes." I could feel his body tense.

"Do you think it's the ghost?"

"I hope so," he replied tersely. We waited, but there was only silence.

After the rattling stopped, it was sort of cool to think the ghost had come to the door. But Levi and I were not prepared for the crazy little screech that came out of thin air beside the bed. We both jumped, then froze. For a few seconds, neither of us spoke. Finally, I asked Levi if there was a radiator in the room. He reached out in the dark and felt a radiator beside the bed, but it wasn't hot. The high-pitched shrieky sound started up again and continued, a nonsensical NEE NEENEENEE NENEEN-NEEE! Whatever it was, it sounded perturbed. Then it stopped.

Levi and I were a little stunned. Unlike door rattling or footsteps, this noise seemed raw and emotional. I asked if a spirit was trying to communicate, and the radiator started up again—NEE NEENEENNEEE! Levi and I asked a few questions, uncertain if the weird shrieky sounds were the spirit's responses or just a broken radiator noise. I had the impres-

164

sion we were being treated to an escalating litany of grievances. I have seen and heard ghosts before, but I couldn't tell if this noise was coming from a ghost or not. The ghosts in my house communicate through the radiators, but with whispers, not shrieks. The radiators in my house are from the same era as the ones at the hotel, and they have never made a noise like the one we were hearing. When I spoke on a radio show one day with Mary Ann Winkowski, the real-life ghost whisperer who inspired the television show of the same name, she told me it was common for spirits to use heating and plumbing pipes to communicate.

I wished that I had better clairvoyant or psychic skills so I could either see the spirit or communicate with it more effectively—or see if there was nothing there. I said, "If this is a spirit trying to communicate, please do something else so we know we're not just talking to a radiator." The radiator responded with a loud CLANK! Levi said that was the moment he became convinced we were actually talking to a ghost.

I spent the next five or ten minutes asking questions: "Are you the spirit woman from this room? Are you unhappy? Do you need help? Do you want to go to the light?" The experience reminded me of talking to my cats, trying to figure out what they want through cues other than language—deciphering the timing and tone of their meows and applying a little intuition and deductive reasoning power.

After this sincere attempt at communication, our best guess was that the spirit was not happy, didn't want help, and did not want to go to the light. I thanked the spirit for communicating and asked her to let us get some sleep. After two more brief but quieter shrieky noises, the radiator went silent. I actually got out of bed and knelt down and prayed for peace for the spirit and for the hotel. When I got back in bed, Levi and I talked about how freaky and interesting the experience was. We dozed off but woke up at 6 AM to a SSSSSsssss! coming from the radiator. Levi and I braced ourselves for more caterwauling, but the radiator didn't shriek or do anything else that radiators have no business doing. It just hissed. We got up and went into each room in our PJs, checking the radiators to see if they were all making the same noise. (It was weird, but so much fun, to have the entire place to ourselves to explore in this way. It felt very Scooby Doo-ish, which is how I usually describe my experiences living in a haunted house.) The radiators all seemed to be firing up for the day and we concluded that there must be a timer on the thermostat, and 6 AM was when they were set to warm up the bedrooms. My hat was still sitting on the bed in the middle room where I had left it the night before. It hadn't moved or disappeared and didn't seem to be bewitched in any way, so I picked it up and brought it back to our room.

· · · · · ·

A few months later, I invited my friend Will Barker to join Levi and me at the Trempealeau Blues Bash. When I told him he could stay in a haunted hotel, he started to laugh and said, "Do you remember when I called you from a haunted hotel last year? That was the place!" I did remember getting a phone message about a haunted hotel from Will, but he hadn't left any details. A laconic restaurateur who spends a lot of time sailing or taking road trips on his motorcycle, Will does believe in ghosts and has had a couple of spirit encounters himself. There was a ghost named Walter in the first restaurant Will owned in Hudson. Walter's heavy footsteps could be heard walking across the creaky hardwood floors after the bar and grill was closed for the night and all the customers had gone home.

I asked Will to tell me again what happened to him the night he stayed at the haunted hotel. He said he was completely alone in the place, which was pretty weird to begin with. I asked if he was in room 5, and he said he didn't remember that kind of stuff. He said he slept in the room that faced the river at the end of the hall. "That's room 5!" I practically shouted. Will said he woke up in the night because he thought he heard someone walking around out in the hallway. Then he said the radiator made a crazy noise—spooky, like it was upset about something. He toughed it out till morning, but it was definitely a strange night.

· · · · · ·

After Levi and I had checked the radiators in all the other rooms at the Trempealeau Hotel, we went back to our room and fell asleep again. We woke up around 8 AM. It was daylight. We took our time getting dressed and brushing our teeth in the community bathroom. We gathered up our stuff, said goodbye to the ghost, and lingered for a minute in the room just in case she wanted to communicate one last time. But the room was silent. When we got to the small sitting room at the top of the steps, we heard a clang from somewhere back at the far end of the hallway, a ghostly goodbye, or maybe good riddance, from the occupant of room 5.

A blue jay feather from Dylan.

There are nights when the wolves are
silent and only the moon howls.
George Carlin
❧

The White Deer:
Stories of a Friend

The news of my friend Dylan's death was mysterious and dramatic, which he would have sort of hated and sort of loved. He was a study in opposites—a tall, handsome, sexy mountain man who could be the life of the party or the ruin of it. Dylan was an avid fisherman and a great storyteller, popular with men and irresistible to women. But he could also be intensely private and often just disappeared for days, weeks, even months at a time, battling some great sadness that he didn't want to talk about.

My childhood friend Becky, who had introduced me to Dylan in the early 1980s, called me with the news. It was early, and she woke me up—"What's Dylan's middle name? How old was he? There's an obituary with his name on it! It can't be him, can it?" In shock and still half-asleep, I searched the online obituaries, the computer screen a blur of words that I could barely decipher without my contacts in, until I saw Dylan's name. Over the next hour, I had almost convinced myself that there had to be some mistake—his name was spelled wrong, for one thing—until Becky called back after confirming with other friends that Dylan was gone.

I spent the rest of the day thinking about Dylan and the bond we had shared, and all the experiences we had gone through together, good and bad. We had been in love and had spent time together off and on over the years. It never lasted, but we never got tired of each other either. When we weren't lovers, we were friends. If one of us was involved with a new person, the other wished them well and stayed away. Our relationship went on in this way for nearly twenty years. I felt a strange kinship with Dylan that I hadn't felt with other men. We resonated on some invisible level that we both recognized, even though we couldn't explain it. One winter morning, when I was shoveling my sidewalk, I came across some boot prints in the snow and had an unexpected emotional reaction to them. I didn't want to shovel them away, I wanted to follow them. It turned out the boot prints were Dylan's. I hadn't seen him in months, but he had stopped by late the night before and left a photograph on my front porch, stuck in the plastic bag the newspaper came in. I once wrote a love story about Dylan and me and our strange, powerful bond that made the cover of a local alternative paper. Dylan pretended to be embarrassed by all the attention, but he showed the story to his friends, so I knew he liked it.

When I got the news that Dylan had died, I hadn't seen him for a while, although we usually spoke on the phone a few times a year. I had been in a serious relationship with a sexy and smart scientist named Rex, with whom I expected to spend the rest of my life. Dylan, too, had settled into a happy long-term relationship with someone, and I thought Dylan and I might finally be going our separate ways. When Rex and I ended our relationship after six years, I didn't call Dylan because I didn't want to create any waves in his life. And I had decided after our last very sad and difficult breakup that Dylan and I should remain friends rather than be lovers again.

Two weeks before he died, Dylan called me. His relationship had ended, and things weren't going well. He wanted to get together, but between my schedule and his, we had to put off our visit for three weeks, until early April. Dylan came into town unexpectedly for a doctor appointment in mid-March and left a message on my answering machine. He asked where I was and if I could meet him for lunch. I called back and left him a message, saying I couldn't meet him that day but to call me to set up our April get-together. I was looking forward to seeing Dylan but not looking forward to telling him that I thought we should be friends rather than lovers. But Dylan didn't call back, and I never saw him again.

On the day of Dylan's funeral, we had the first beautiful weather of the year after a long, harsh winter. I felt so bad about everything—about not getting together with Dylan in March; about being out of touch with him for so long; about him being gone from my life forever. The funeral didn't provide much solace, either. It was during Lent, and the pastor gave a fire-and-brimstone homily. He reminded us that we were all sinners—including Dylan and citing him by name—and said that only God's mercy would save us. The memorial service program had a typo and instead of Dylan's name, it said Herb. Becky had brought along a small travel pack of deluxe tissues with angels on them, but we were both so unmoved by the service that we never even cried. At one point, I leaned over to Becky and whispered, "I hope Dylan isn't watching this." She nodded and whispered back, "He's probably fishing somewhere. And laughing at us for being stuck in here." After the church service, we walked across the hall to the community room, where I read a poem I had written for Dylan. Becky and I told his family how sorry we were, and left. When I got home, I sat on my back steps and cried for two hours. I told Dylan how sorry I was and everything else I needed to tell him.

It was during my farewell cry-a-thon to Dylan that I decided to find my notes about seeing Dylan's white deer one night in a vision. I went up to my room and got out my old datebooks, which I always hang on to because I record my dreams and weird experiences in them. More than once in the years I knew him, Dylan had told the story of seeing a mysterious white deer. He saw the deer in northern Wisconsin, and somewhere in Alaska when he was up working on the fishing boats, and once when he was living in Nebraska. I thought the white deer had to be something mystical, but Dylan laughed at the idea, saying, "Voodoo and chicken bones! I don't believe in that stuff." He did acknowledge that it was weird that he had seen a white deer in such far-flung places, but he insisted it was a real deer. I told him it must be his totem animal, at least. Dylan seemed to like the idea of having a totem animal, and we left it at that.

I thought my white deer vision had taken place a few years earlier, but when I looked through my datebooks, I discovered I had seen it only eleven months before Dylan died. At the time, I was using a bedroom (now the playroom) in my house that we don't generally use as a bedroom anymore because of all the weird haunting activity that has happened in it. On the night of the vision, I woke up and saw a glowing light coming in from the window. In the light stood a white deer. I knew immediately it was Dylan's white deer. The most memorable thing about the deer was how real it looked. Its coat was dull and a little scruffy, and it had dried mud on its fetlock. When I saw the dried mud, I thought to myself, "Dylan was right! It is real." The week that I saw the white deer was a very active week at my house from an astral perspective. Within a three-day period, along with seeing the white deer, I had three unusual precognitive dreams. After living in a haunted house for fifteen years, I have noticed that astral and ghost activity generally follow a pattern. Things will escalate, reach a peak, and then quiet down again. I didn't associate seeing the deer with any particular danger or message about Dylan. I thought it was just a cool experience, another facet of the mysterious connection Dylan and I shared. I did try to call Dylan just to check in, but the last number I had for him was no longer in service. Dylan called me three days later. It was the first time we had chatted in months. He didn't know what to think about me seeing the white deer, but he said everything was fine.

. . . . . .

I have had a few cool dreams about Dylan since he's been gone, mostly variations of the experiences we shared when he was alive. In one dream,

I was at a cabin he had lived in decades earlier. Dylan wasn't there—no one was—but on the counter, I found a note he had left me. It said, "I'm sorry" and "I love you."

I also had a spirit visit from Dylan on a night when I needed his help. There was some strange and threatening ghostly activity howling through my house on the astral level. I came to this conclusion because, within the space of four nights, I had two very disturbing nightmares involving witches, and the nightmares were like a continuing dream that was escalating in danger. I usually find witches to be a positive symbol in my dreams, but these particular witches were up to no good. In the first nightmare, I dreamt that I woke up and saw four witches standing at the foot of my bed. The witches were not doing anything, but I definitely picked up a predatory vibe. The first witch's face was rotting flesh. The second witch's hair was covering her face. The third's hat was covering her face. The fourth witch's dress was a shiny metallic gray color. I never saw her face, because at that point I woke up panting with fear.

Four nights later, the witches were back. In the second dream, angry witches were flying through my house. I actually woke up to loud, hollow pounding noises reverberating through my house. The experience started with me dreaming that I took a different route home from work, through the vintage, blue-collar east side of St. Paul. The streets were narrow, and the old houses in the rundown neighborhood of my dream all had life-sized witch decorations on their porches. The witches were hanging upside down, still on their brooms. Their heads were rolled back so people passing by could see their faces. I was thinking how very scary they were when the witch decoration I was looking at shifted her eyes to look directly at me. A terrible feeling of dread came over me as all the witches, still upside down, started to swing slowly back and forth. I realized they were alive and wanted to get free. The next thing I knew, I was back in my house. Witches were flying around at breakneck speed. Suddenly Dylan appeared beside me, standing next to the couch. (I was sleeping in the living room when I had this dream, because it was an extremely hot night in the summertime, and I wanted to be near the air conditioner.) When I saw Dylan, relief washed over me and I felt safe, like everything was going to be okay. I knew Dylan was a spirit, but the whole experience felt really practical and solid, like a friend helping a friend rather than something emotional or transcendent. That's when I woke up and actually heard the loud pounding noises. I felt braver and better equipped to deal with whatever was going on because of Dylan's spirit visit. (I never did come up with a satisfactory answer to what caused the astral disturbances that week.)

I had another dream about Dylan about a year after he died that felt like more than a dream. In it, I was visiting Red Wing, Minnesota, a beautiful old city on the Mississippi River with steep, winding streets and grand historic homes. I was a passenger in a car, and I saw Dylan walking on the sidewalk. He was hand in hand with a young woman with long brown hair. My heart leapt; I was so happy and surprised to see him. I told the driver to stop the car. I ran up to Dylan and grabbed him, squeezing his arms in disbelief and saying, "Dylan, I'm so happy to see you! Everyone thought you had died!"

Dylan looked into my eyes. He smiled, but there was some new distance between us, a boundary that I had never felt before. With uncharacteristic earnestness, he said, "Annie, I needed a rest." I could see traces of exhaustion in Dylan's face, but I could also see an unfamiliar serenity. I knew then that he had died, and I was seeing his spirit. I said, "I understand, Dylan. I understand. You did need a rest." I hugged him tightly; it felt so good to hold him again. I returned to the car that was waiting for me. As I looked back, Dylan and the young woman were walking away. I realized with a start that the woman walking away with Dylan was me, when I was about twenty. That's how old I was when Dylan and I met.

Thinking about it the next day, I wondered if the dream had actually been me visiting Dylan in the spirit world, in the same way my Irish family spirits occasionally come visit me in the physical world. But if so, why did I find a younger version of myself there? I've been told by more than one psychic that most of my spirit energy is not in my body, and that's why astral travel and seeing ghosts comes more easily to me than to many people. Maybe it has to do with soul loss, like my mom losing part of her spirit at age five. Dylan and I had both been through some extremely difficult times in our lives, together and before we met. Maybe some broken-off parts of our spirits were hanging out together in the astral world, and that's why we had such a lasting bond in the physical world. I had always thought the white deer was some sort of guardian spirit for Dylan. But after hearing about my mom's experience with the ghost girl, I have come to believe that the white deer may have been part of Dylan's own spirit, wild and free, waiting to reunite with him on this side or the other.

For Dylan

I SEE by the notice in the paper
I spelled your name wrong all these years
You always were like a ghost anyway
a phone call from nowhere
a letter in the mailbox with no return address
slipping into and out of my life like a wraith
It was only in my imagination that I could get you to sit still
calm your restlessness, keep you safe
When you'd show up on my doorstep
could you feel how pleased I was?
Your strong arms holding me tight
that hair I loved to touch
I can close my eyes and remember it all
I tried to tie you to life with kisses and desire
wrap up some happiness to send with you on your way
get you to stay a little longer

You never liked to leave tracks
a blue jay feather you gave me one April
a note you left on my counter in 1986
these are the only keepsakes I have
You told me the story of a white deer you had seen in the woods
different times and different places in your life
laughed when I said it was a sign
The white deer—did it come for you, Dylan?
Lead you to a trout brook that sparkles and sings
Dylan, kindred spirit, lover, and friend
there has always been a haven for you
in my heart and my imagination
I hope you will visit me there from time to time

Front to back: Mimi, Grandma Dorrie, and Nellie in front of
the Irish family homestead, St. Paul, Minnesota, circa 1925.

> In every loving woman there is a priestess of
> the past—a pious guardian of some affection,
> of which the object has disappeared.
> *Henri Frederic Amiel*

Farewell,
Irish Family Homestead

Six or seven years ago, I walked through the Irish family home, awash in memories and the vibrations of the past. It was the first time I had been in my great-grandma Maggie's house, now Great-Aunt Irene's, in nearly thirty years. The days of the house overflowing with Irish relatives, neighbors, and friends were long gone. Great-Grandma, Mimi, Big Uncle Thomas, Big Luke, Grandma Dorrie, Norah, and Nellie had all passed away. But they were also still there, my Irish relatives, or at least traces of their energy were—their daily sorrows and joys lingered in the house long after their days on earth were done. The house was so filled with spirit energy, I had to stop and collect myself before I could go beyond the first two rooms. Norah's daughter Kay had asked if I could take Great-Aunt Irene out for their usual Friday night dinner date, as she was going to be out of town and wouldn't be available. I saw Irene at all of our family parties, of course, but the party hosting had moved on to the next generation and other houses. The Irish family homestead had gotten quiet.

The back screened porch, where Big Uncle Thomas used to watch ball games on the television with his Irish setter Prince by his side, now had two lawn chairs so Irene could enjoy a cup of coffee and watch the birds with her guests. The porch still had the sixties-era indoor-outdoor green carpeting that I remembered. The kitchen, which for decades had been the center of activity for so many family gatherings, seemed tiny. The historic neighborhood, which had been a stable and safe working-class community in its heyday, was now in decline.

In the fall of 2004, my daughter Molly, who was in her mid-twenties, moved into the Irish home with Great-Aunt Irene. Irene was Big Uncle Thomas's widow and the last family member of her generation still living. At ninety-four, Irene was still sharp and funny, but she needed someone around to help out if she was going to be able to stay in her home. Irene did have helpers coming in five days a week, but due to having surgery, she needed someone there overnight as well. My mom's sister Margie and cousin Kay, along with one of Irene's nieces from her side of the family, devoted a lot of time to helping Irene continue to live in her home. My aunt Margie had finally convinced Irene to update the house a bit, using some of her favorite colors. The living and dining room carpeting, which had been emerald green, Uncle Thomas's favorite color, was replaced with a soft rose-colored carpet. Margie had also helped Irene purchase some new furniture that was comfortable and pretty.

Irene had been at a nursing home while recuperating from surgery, but she hated it so much that she tried to bribe one of the employees into taking her home. When that didn't work, she attempted to leave by calling a taxi and offering to pay the driver in jewelry. Irene had lived in the Irish family home for almost seventy years, and she had only lived in one other house her entire life, so it was easy to see why she was so intent on getting back to her house. I was proud of Molly for being part of an endeavor so important and worthwhile. And I was glad Molly was strong and practical and used to living with spirits. I figured she would probably encounter a few in her time at the Irish house.

So Molly moved in, bringing her three cats with her. We had been a little concerned about the cats with Irene's mobility issues, but Irene fell in love with them. Molly's tiny cat, Snip, was Irene's favorite. Snip, who does whatever she wants, would ride around in the basket of Irene's walker, sticking her chest out like a ship's figurehead. Occasionally, Molly would come home from work and discover that Irene had created little trails of food leading to her chair to get Snip to come sit in her lap.

Molly moved into the upstairs bedroom that had belonged to Great-Aunt Mimi for more than fifty years. She told me sometimes at night when she was in bed, she would hear strange noises and think of all of the relatives who had lived in the house, and Big Luke, who had died there. One night, Molly had a dream in which she thought she woke up. She heard heavy footsteps coming up the stairs and then felt like something was in her room with her, pinning her down. Molly said even in the dream, she didn't think it was Big Luke's spirit, but she thought it was a male spirit who had lived in the house. She got the distinct impression that the angry spirit wanted her boyfriend Bryan to stop coming around. Molly had another vivid dream that was a little spooky, but mostly cool. She dreamt that she woke up and heard a party going on downstairs. She went down to check it out, and found the living and dining room packed with youngish but old-fashioned partygoers, drinking and eating and playing cards. They looked like they were from the 1940s or '50s. No one seemed to notice her, and she went back upstairs.

Energetically speaking, Molly said she felt the strongest sense of the past in the old basement, where she felt a residual vibe of parties and gaiety. Molly did not see any ghosts while living in the house, but she and Irene both heard voices at night. The voices were muffled—neither Molly nor Irene could understand what they were saying. One night, Molly came home late, and Irene was upset because while Molly was out, Irene had heard a loud knock. They both had the death knock on their minds as Molly went around the house to see if she could find anything that had fallen over or was out of place, but she found nothing.

Molly's favorite part of living with Irene was listening to the stories she told about her life. When Molly found an old shoebox full of photographs, she and Irene looked through the pictures together. One photo was of Big Uncle Thomas petting Prince in the living room, right where she and Irene were sitting. There were a few photos in which the "old" relatives were unrecognizable to Molly because they were young. In one of them, four people Molly didn't recognize were sitting at a table drinking, smoking, and playing cards. Irene laughed and told Molly that it was her, Mimi, Big Uncle Thomas, and a neighbor. Molly said she loved listening to Irene's stories because it was obvious that while she told the stories, she was reliving them. According to Molly, who wrote a paper about the experience for grad school:

> *Irene would get very emotionally caught up in her story, a few times she cried, but most of the time she laughed and smiled during the story and after the story. I know she enjoyed telling me the stories, especially those that ended with her sighing and saying, "Just imagine." I did imagine the stories she told me. When I was doing laundry in the basement, I would imagine thirty adults in the back room drinking at the homemade bar, and I imagined Big Luke falling asleep in his chair while reading a book and never waking up.*

I believe that, even though the Irish family home had gotten much quieter, there was still some fairy magic left around. In the same week I saw the vision of my friend Dylan's white deer, I dreamt I was at a big family party at my grandparents' house. As I looked around, I suddenly realized that everyone seated at the table was a ghost. One of the women became aware that I knew she was a spirit and tried to fly away. I yelled out, "Name yourself!" As she disappeared into the ceiling, she called back, "Eileen Gallagher," who was one of the family friends that had been part of our parties for decades. I wrote the dream down in my datebook. About a week later, I went to visit Irene and found a picture lying on the floor of a woman from the 1960s. I picked it up and showed it to Irene. I asked who it was, and Irene said, "That's Eileen Gallagher." I said, "Oh, how weird! I just had a dream about her a week ago!" Irene asked me if I remembered Eileen. I told her I remembered Eileen Gallagher, Bridget Flanagan, and Margaret Brennan (whose mother was the woman who went blind when she saw her daughter struck by a street car), who all came to the parties, even though, as a kid, I wasn't sure exactly who they were. (I even remembered people referring obliquely to Bridget's sister Babe, who we weren't supposed to talk about. I never found out why, except that she was "wild.") I asked Irene where the picture of Eileen Gallagher had come from. She said she didn't know—it had just shown up that morning.

The other item that just showed up one day on Irene's end table was a man's gold watch. Irene showed it to me the next time I came over. She asked me what I thought it meant. "Hmmm ..." I thought about it. It seemed a little ominous, given Irene's age. I searched for a more positive interpretation. "Maybe the fairies are back?"

I asked Irene what she was going to do with the watch.

"I'm just watching it," Irene said, smiling at her own play on words. "I'm curious to see what it's going to do next."

Once Irene learned that I lived in a haunted house, she started telling me about some of the weird things she had experienced in her house. I know some people think that older people are confused or their medications are playing tricks on them, and I know that may be true in some situations. But I also believe that the closer we get to the end of our physical life, the more awareness and interaction we have with the spirit world. The first weird thing that Irene told me about was her blanket standing up beside the bed. She woke up one night because she was cold. She figured she must have accidentally knocked her blanket to the floor, but then she saw the blanket standing straight up in the air beside her bed. Irene referred to that story many times, because it had absolutely shocked her.

Irene also told me that on more than one occasion, she woke up and saw little people, or fairies, going through her dresser drawers, and she wasn't happy about it. I told her about Dan's Irish renter, who believed that brownies were straightening up the pile of shoes and boots by his back door at night, and suggested that maybe the little people were helping her keep her clothes in order.

Irene's most dramatic ghostly encounter was waking up and seeing a "craggy-faced" man beside her bed. And—I love this part, because Irene was in her nineties at the time—she didn't scream, and she didn't cower under her covers. She hit him, which I think is a perfectly appropriate response to seeing a menacing stranger standing beside your bed.

"That's so righteous!" I told Irene when I first heard the story. "Then what happened? Did he disappear?"

"My hand went right through him," said Irene. "Then he disappeared."

Irene also talked about a "spirit man, come to dance me away." I thought it was a poetic and powerful way to refer to dying. But I wasn't sure if Irene was actually referring to death, and because of her age, I felt it would be bad manners to ask her directly. I got the answer when Molly moved in with Irene. When Molly greeted Irene in the morning and asked her how she was doing, Irene would often smile and reply, "The spirit man didn't come to dance me away last night, so I'm fine."

Molly had to get up early during the week to go to work. Since Irene was a night owl, often staying up very late to watch TV, Molly tried to be unobtrusive when she came downstairs, keeping the lights off and walking quietly. One morning, as Molly came down the staircase, she froze. She could see Irene's figure silhouetted in her chair in the dark living room. With her heart in her throat, Molly braced herself to go over and check on Irene, when Irene suddenly chirped, "Good morning!"

Molly's knees buckled. She said it was the closest she's ever come to collapsing from fear. When she caught her breath, she said, "Irene, what are you doing sitting in the dark?"

Irene said, "I was hoping you could teach me how to use the microwave oven." Everyone had been trying to get Irene to stop using the stove, so it was a perfectly reasonable request, although Molly was still quaking inside when she got to work a half-hour later.

Molly and her cats lived with Irene for about a year. A painful chronic spinal condition finally made it necessary for Irene to move into a nursing home. When I visited Irene in the nursing home, it broke my heart when she leaned over to me and said, "Say, can you tell me about my house? I'm forgetting what it looks like."

Molly lived in St. Paul for a year, then moved to Savannah, Georgia, to attend grad school. I had a new cigarette-smoking ghost at my house, and Molly dreamt that she met the spirit. It was an old woman with bright red hair, wearing dark sunglasses. The woman had a lit cigarette in her mouth and was taking boxes out of my house. When Molly asked her what she was doing, the woman turned around, took off her sunglasses, and said, "I'm helping your mother sell books." As soon as Molly saw the old woman's eyes, which were red-rimmed, she knew she was talking to a ghost. I thought there was a good chance the spirit was Mimi, since she looked like Mimi, was helping with books (which were Mimi's life work), and Molly had just spent a year sleeping in Mimi's old room, so they probably had an energetic connection. It also seemed to me that Mimi's eyes had always been a little red, but I couldn't remember for sure. We asked my mom if Mimi had been a smoker, and she said, "Oh, yes. Everyone smoked then." We also asked her about red-rimmed eyes, and she said that between Mimi's coloring (red hair and very fair skin) and the eyestrain from her job, her eyes often did look red. I always think my Irish relatives are helping from the other side, and Molly's dream was just another confirmation of that, so I thanked Mimi for the help. And I have not experienced any more ghostly cigarette smoke at my house since then.

A few years ago, when it became apparent that Irene would not ever be able to go back to her home, the Irish family home was put on the market and sold. I have to keep reminding myself that a house is not part of the family, it's just a place that holds a family's spirit for a while. And I believe that houses have a life cycle, just like people do. Our Irish family home is gone from us, but new again for some other family. May they have many happy times there.

My most heart-wrenching moment in the Irish homestead was when I helped Molly move some of her stuff into the basement on the day she moved in, and I saw the bar that my great-grandpa had built in the back corner. I knew that Maggie and Thomas had moved into the house shortly after the terrible year in which Annie, Ethel, and James had died, hoping to make a fresh start in a new home. As I gazed at the long-deserted bar in a now-dark corner of the basement, the jaunty red ribbon painted around it moved me to tears. It made me realize what incredible resiliency and strength and hope my great-grandparents possessed. It also made me realize that when my grandma Dorrie had a basement bar built in her beautiful historic home, and Norah set up a basement bar for all the family parties, they were following a family tradition that they knew fostered happiness and joy.

My mom recently had a vision of Great-Aunt Mimi. She had been listening to André Rieu on PBS, and they were playing a Viennese waltz. My mom suddenly saw a very distinct image of Mimi dancing to a Strauss waltz, which she had always loved to do. Mimi was wearing a beautiful ball gown. My mom didn't recognize her partner, but I bet it was Fred, the man Mimi had loved but didn't marry because of his parents' objections. Mimi and Fred had found each other again, later in life, when he became a widower. They were planning a trip to Europe when Mimi was diagnosed with cancer. She died not long afterward. Everyone felt very sad that, once again, circumstances had kept Mimi and Fred apart. But in my mom's psychic impression of Mimi dancing, she said it was easy to see that Mimi was supremely happy.

I have no doubt all the Irish relatives in spirit are together, celebrating and helping out from the other side when they're needed. In my first book, I wrote about a conversation I had with my grandma Dorrie, with a little help from psychic Patrick Mathews. At the end of the reading, I reluctantly said goodbye to my grandma. She told Patrick that she had a luncheon to attend with a bunch of the family on the other side, which is exactly how I picture my Irish relatives enjoying their time in heaven, in between dropping by to visit or help.

There will never be another generation of people quite like my grandparents and great-grandparents. Thankfully, it is likely that none of us will have to endure the kinds of heartbreaking losses and hardships they endured. When my young nieces and nephews and cousins are old enough, we will share the family stories with them so they can be inspired by their ancestors and, in some small way, get to know them. In the meantime, I always greet the rabbits in my yard with a friendly hello and set out bread crusts for them, just in case Great-Grandma Maggie was right.

Of course that is not the whole story, but that is the way with stories; we make them what we will. It's a way of explaining the universe while leaving the universe unexplained, it's a way of keeping it all alive, not boxing it into time.

Jeanette Winterson

Afterword

On the long winter nights when I was immersed in writing this book, I often felt our family spirits around me. One February night, my son Jack came in at 2:30 in the morning and, as he unlocked the back door, heard a man whistling in the summer kitchen. When Jack stepped inside the house, the summer kitchen was empty and dark. When I heard Jack's story, I asked my mom and dad if any of our relatives were known for whistling. My dad said his father, Grandpa Morgan, loved to whistle but couldn't anymore after having the tumor removed from his lip back in the 1930s. I had just finished the Montana Ghosts chapter, so I interpreted the whistling as a message from Grandpa Morgan, a friendly and distinctive way for him to let us know he was here for a visit and he was happy about the book project—and that he can whistle once again.

This past Memorial Day weekend, my parents and some of us kids and grandkids went down to southern Minnesota for a remembrance picnic, inspired by a recent conversation I had with Great-Aunt Clara for this book. My folks showed us the Schultz and Wieland family homesteads, which we had heard about but never seen. We stopped on the hill where Great-Great-Grandpa Schultz's horse team had fallen on the snowy night in 1896 when my great-grandparents met. We visited the cemetery and went to our old farm and the church where my parents were married. We drove past Grandma and Grandpa Haraldson's house, stopped at the town drug store for a soda, and did a walking tour of the street where Great-Grandma and Great-Grandpa Schultz and other family members and friends had lived. We brought our genealogy books and old pictures to show the kids what it was like when we were young and when our mom and dad were young. We spent the day exploring and remembering our history.

Stories are gifts. They reveal our past, and the past is part of who we are, whether it is invisible to us or known. I am fortunate that people took the time here and there to jot down stories and save cards and letters, and that my uncle Larry and aunt Margie organized these stories and vignettes into more permanent documents that we can add to as time goes by.

Every family's story is interesting and special. I hope this book inspires people to see the magic in their own experiences and to write down their family stories.

Rituals to Protect Yourself
and Bless Your Space

E ach of us is an energy steward, responsible for our personal energy and the energy of our environment. I believe that positive energy is the best defense against negativity in any form, including negative spirits.

Protecting Yourself

There are many ways to keep your personal energy positive, and the simplest is to make sure you spend your time with people you care about, doing things you love. Love is the most powerful energy there is, especially if you're going through difficult times.

Moving energy through your body is another way to keep your energy field strong and clear. From practicing qi gong or yoga to dancing, gardening, or walking the dog, there are a variety of enjoyable ways to keep your energy flowing. I've found that the energy healing practice of Reiki is a great way to channel positive energy for myself and for others. When psychic C. J. Sellers came through my house during a film shoot, she walked into my bedroom with a smile and said, "I feel the Reiki energy in this room." That made me happy, as I do think my room has a really positive vibe. And since I start nearly every day with Reiki prayers before I even get out of bed, I was pleased that C. J. had tuned in to the Reiki energy. C. J. also asked me if I saw spirits outside my room at night, because she was picking up a lot of spirit energy in the hallway. I said yes. She told me that, as a sign of respect, they (mostly) stay out of my room.

Earlier in this book, I referred to shielding techniques, which are ways to protect yourself on the astral level. Envisioning a big iron curtain around myself was a natural, basic form of shielding. There is an excellent book out called *The Ghost Hunter's Survival Guide* by Michelle Belanger, which focuses entirely on shielding and other techniques for protecting oneself from negative spirits and astral beings, if you find yourself in a situation that requires more than the basic techniques I offer here. (The book is listed in the recommended reading section as well.)

I myself use a combination of prayer, Reiki energy, and calling on my family and allies in the spirit world for assistance when I feel threatened or scared. Actually, I often ask my family spirits or Leon, the primary protective spirit for my house, for their assistance on things ranging from helping a family member through a health crisis to giving me a hand in getting the lawn mower started. When my young cousin Alexandra was living with me as she struggled with the difficult decision of whether to keep her baby Shea or place her for adoption, I was praying to my grandma Dorrie and all of our Irish relatives in spirit—Great-Grandma Maggie, Mimi, Big Uncle Thomas, and Nellie. One morning, shortly before Alexandra made the decision to place her baby for adoption with a wonderful family, I heard a whispered message: "There are five of us helping you." And I knew my family was helping from the other side.

Blessing Your Space

The same principles that keep your personal energy positive and strong apply to your living space. I used to clean houses for a living, and I found that homes that had companion animals, plants or flowers, original artwork (usually done by children), and photographs of people they cared about generally felt much more positive and nurturing than homes that were lacking these things. If you keep your house clean and uncluttered (but not bare) and fill it with things that make you happy, you'll have a great foundation for keeping your home protected from unwelcome negative astral visitors. Taking care of something is a way of connecting with it. I am tuned in to my house, and that helps me become aware of any astral blips or aberrations that might be the harbinger of bigger ghostly problems.

At least once or twice a year, it's a good idea to bless and cleanse your home. First, do a regular cleaning. Then open the windows as you move from room to room with holy water or sage (the sage can be unlit if you don't like the smell of burning sage). Ask for the house to be protected and blessed, and for all negative energy to leave through the open windows and to dissipate in the atmosphere. This is also good to do if a traumatic event has occurred. After my neighbor Wolf got badly hurt using a table saw, he and his brother and I had a small sageing ceremony in his garage, where the accident took place. Afterward, we each had a shot of tequila to celebrate Wolf's recovery and talked about Australia, where his brother lives and where Wolf was going to visit.

If you feel that stronger actions are required to protect your space, consider putting a pinch of salt in the corner of each room and placing religious or otherwise spiritually meaningful icons in each room as well. The day after one of the most frightening experiences I've ever had at home, I walked through my entire house, singing loudly. I had read that singing is a shamanic technique for transforming energy. I also wanted to prove to myself (and to any astral beings that might have lingered) that I wasn't afraid. After singing, I walked through the house burning sage and asking for blessings and protection for the house and all positive people, animals, and spirits that live here.

Take the time occasionally to walk through your house or look around your work area, and appreciate how fortunate you are to have a home and a job. Next to love, I think gratitude is one of the most powerful forms of energy there is. A space filled with positive energy is not going to be attractive to negative astral beings, but it will be an environment in which creativity and happiness can flourish.

A Ritual to Honor
Your Family in Spirit

One of the things I regretted after my grandma Dorrie passed away was that our mega-social family never held a party just to thank my grandma and Great-Aunt Norah and their siblings for all they had done for us and all the happy times they created.

In his book *Never Say Goodbye*, psychic Patrick Mathews says that even after loved ones die, we still have a relationship with them. The relationship changes, but it doesn't disappear. I'm pretty good at chatting with my grandma Dorrie and her siblings, especially Norah and Nellie, who I knew best, and my Montana grandparents, Dylan, Leon, and any other friendly spirit when I need their help or think they may have stopped by to visit. But I got the idea of doing something a little more formal to connect with my family in spirit when I read about a ritual called the Dumb Supper. It's a rite many cultures use to honor the dead. Held on Halloween, it's a solemn and silent affair in which the table is draped in black, and a plate is set for the deceased person. As cool and powerful as this ritual sounds, it didn't seem like a good fit for the happy, buzzy energy that characterizes our family parties. But it gave me an idea.

I put together an invitation and mailed it to all our Irish family relatives. Here's what it said:

All Souls' Day Eve Remembrance and Storytelling Circle

Share stories, dreams, visits, transcendent experiences,
and remembrances of family and friends in spirit.

We gathered at 7 PM at my house. I put a candleholder that I call the storyteller candle on my table. My girlfriend Becky gave me this candleholder. It's a clay sculpture with faces carved in a circle. A tea light sits on a pedestal in the middle and casts flickering light on the faces. Everyone brought photographs or mementos and set them on the table. As we were setting things up, people spontaneously shared stories and admired family pictures they hadn't seen before.

We poured beverages and went into the living room. Sitting in a circle, we toasted our family and friends in spirit, thanking them for the love they showed us and the lessons we learned from them. Then we started telling stories. It was here that I learned some of the events of my great-grandma Maggie's life that appear in this book. After laughing and crying together, we gathered in the kitchen to eat and visit some more before people left for home. This wasn't an attempt to try to contact our family in spirit (although I think that's cool, too). We knew they were already present and part of the celebration.

Afterward, I decided the only things I would do differently in the future would be to have some music or singing as part of the celebration, and better lighting, since a few of my aunts and cousins had a hard time seeing the pictures in the dramatic, subdued lighting. Overall, I think it was a powerful and moving way to remember and honor our family on the other side. What's important, if you decide to hold a remembrance celebration, is to work with your family's style and traditions, incorporating the elements that feel familiar and right to you.

❦

Little Orphant Annie§

James Whitcomb Riley (1849–1916)

INSCRIBED WITH ALL FAITH AND AFFECTION

To all the little children—The happy ones; and sad ones;
The sober and the silent ones; the boisterous and glad ones;
The good ones—Yes, the good ones, too; and all the lovely bad ones.

LITTLE ORPHANT ANNIE'S come to our house to stay,
An' wash the cups an' saucers up, an' brush the crumbs away,
An' shoo the chickens off the porch, an' dust the hearth, an' sweep,
An' make the fire, an' bake the bread, an' earn her board-an'-keep;
An' all us other childern, when the supper-things is done,
We set around the kitchen fire an' has the mostest fun
A-list'nin' to the witch-tales 'at Annie tells about,

---

§ "Little Orphant Annie" is reprinted from *The Complete Works of James Whitcomb Riley* (Indianapolis: Bobbs-Merrill, 1916).

❦

An' the Gobble-uns 'at gits you

    Ef you

        Don't

            Watch

                OUT!

Wunst they wuz a little boy wouldn't say his prayers,

An' when he went to bed at night, away up-stairs,

His Mammy heerd him holler, an' his Daddy heerd him bawl,

An' when they turn't the kivvers down, he wuzn't there at all!

An' they seeked him in the rafter-room, an' cubby-hole, an' press,

An' seeked him up the chimbly-flue, an' ever'-wheres, I guess;

But all they ever found wuz thist his pants an' roundabout:

An' the Gobble-uns 'll git you

    Ef you

        Don't

            Watch

                OUT!

An' one time a little girl 'ud allus laugh an' grin,

An' make fun of ever' one, an' all her blood-an'-kin;

An' wunst, when they was "company," an' ole folks wuz there,

She mocked 'em an' shocked 'em, an' said she didn't care!

An' thist as she kicked her heels, an' turn't to run an' hide,

They wuz two great big Black Things a-standin' by her side,

An' they snatched her through the ceilin' 'fore she knowed what she's about!

An' the Gobble-uns 'll git you

    Ef you

        Don't

            Watch

                OUT!

An' little Orphant Annie says, when the blaze is blue,
An' the lamp-wick sputters, an' the wind goes woo-oo!
An' you hear the crickets quit, an' the moon is gray,
An' the lightnin'-bugs in dew is all squenched away,
You better mind yer parunts, an' yer teachurs fond an' dear,
An' churish them 'at loves you, an' dry the orphant's tear,
An' he'p the pore an' needy ones 'at clusters all about,
Er the Gobble-uns 'll git you
    Ef you
        Don't
            Watch
                OUT!

Astral projection: The experience of one's spirit, or consciousness, leaving the physical body while retaining full awareness and self-knowledge.

Astral vision: The ability to see all sides of an object at once.

Aura: The energy field that surrounds the physical body.

Automatic writing: The process of allowing a spirit to communicate through a medium via a computer, typewriter, or pen and paper.

Banshee: Fearsome spirits whose keening and wailing presage the death of someone in the family.

Brownies: Helpful but capricious house spirits.

Death coach: An old-fashioned spectral hearse that comes to collect the souls of the dead.

Dissociation: The perception of being outside of one's physical body; perceiving one's own body in the role of an observer. Generally a coping response to extreme stress or trauma.

Etheric vision: The ability to see through opaque objects.

Homeopathy: A form of healing that seeks to remedy the energetic origins of disease, rather than treating physical symptoms.

Leprechaun: The clever fairies that delight in outsmarting humans.

Out-of-Body Experience, or OBE: Another term for astral projection.

Portal: A point of entry and exit between the physical and spirit worlds.

Reiki: A form of healing energy.

Scrying: A form of divination in which the querent gazes into a reflective surface such as a mirror or body of water to gain insight into the present or future.

Soul loss: The shamanistic theory that a portion of our soul's energy can break off due to trauma or grief and remain stuck in a certain time or place. Shamanically speaking, soul loss is viewed as contributing to illness and bad luck, as well as being a significant factor in not having sufficient energy to fulfill our soul's purpose for this lifetime.

Soul retrieval: The process of restoring a person's spirit energy by gathering up their lost soul parts and returning the parts to them. A soul retrieval is done through shamanic journeying.

Thought form: A form, usually inanimate, that exists on the astral plane. When a thought form becomes animated, or develops a will of its own, it's called a tulpa.

RECOMMENDED READING

Animal Speak by Ted Andrews (Llewellyn, 1996)

Ecoshamanism by James Endredy (Llewellyn, 2005)

The Ghost Hunter's Survival Guide by Michelle Belanger (Llewellyn, 2009)

The Happy Medium by Jodi Livon (Llewellyn, 2009)

Natural Healing for Dogs & Cats by Diane Stein (Crossing Press, 1993)

Never Say Goodbye by Patrick Mathews (Llewellyn, 2003)

Reaching Through the Veil to Heal by Linda Drake (Llewellyn, 2006)

Relax, It's Only a Ghost by Echo Bodine (Fair Winds Press, 2001)

The Secret Life of Nature by Peter Tompkins (HarperOne, 1997)

Soul Retrieval by Sandra Ingerman (HarperOne, revised, updated edition 2006; originally published by HarperSanFrancisco, 1991)

Twenty Cases Suggestive of Reincarnation by Dr. Ian Stevenson (University Press of Virginia, 1980)

The Way of the Shaman by Michael Harner, Ph.D. (HarperOne, 1990)

Where Reincarnation and Biology Intersect by Dr. Ian Stevenson (Praeger Paperback, 1997)

INDEX

H ere are some of my favorite photographs of the people and places I write about in *Spirits Out of Time*.

The Yellow Eyes

Me and Betsy, circa 1966.

Ottawa, Minnesota, 1965.
Left to right: Betsy, me, and Randall in costume.

Me and my siblings at Grandma and Grandpa Haraldson's
house in southern Minnesota, 1965. Left to right:
Thomas, me, Iris, Betsy, and Randall.

Big Uncle Thomas and his wife Irene in
the driveway of the Irish family home,
St. Paul, Minnesota, circa 1940.

Great-Grandma Maggie, Big Uncle Thomas, and me
(with Cracker Jacks) at a family party, St. Paul, 1967.

Back row, left to right: Grandma Dorrie, Great-Aunt Mimi, Great-Aunt Norah; front: Big Uncle Thomas and Great-Aunt Nellie at a family wedding, circa 1975.

Montana Ghosts

My dad with his great-grandma Tiny Gramma and his grandpa David Morgan at the South Farm, Willard, Montana, 1933.

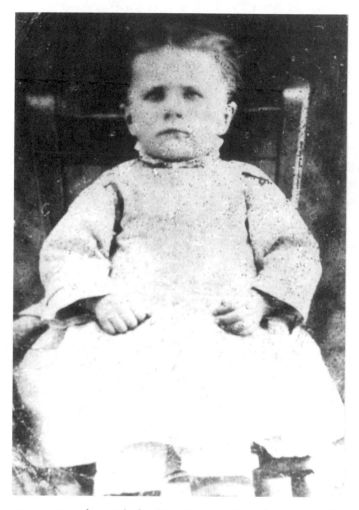

Great-Grandma Schultz (Great-Great-Grandma Wieland's daughter) as a baby in southern Minnesota, circa 1879.

(left) Great-Great-Grandma Wieland and her son, Uncle
Henry, on their southern Minnesota farm, 1922 or '23.
(right) Great-Aunt Clara and Uncle Henry on the Wieland
farm (these two photos were taken on the same day).

My grandpa Bernard
and grandma
Mae (Schultz)
Morgan, Montana,
early 1930s.

My dad (center) with his siblings
Larry and Sister, Montana, 1938.

(Bottom, front)
Great-Grandma and
Grandpa Schultz and
his sisters Margaret
(left) and Emma
(back) in southern
Minnesota, 1965.
(Great-Grandma
is the baby from
page 211.)

My brothers and sisters and me on Grandma and
Grandpa Morgan's front porch in North Dakota with
our cowboy cousins (Uncle Larry and Aunt Connie's
kids). I'm in the back row, second from left.

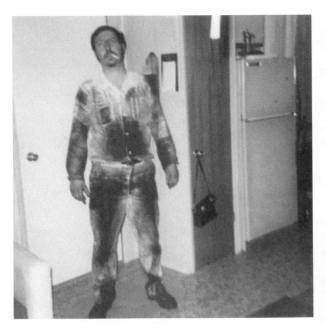

Uncle Jim (my dad's youngest
brother) arriving home
from work, circa 1971.

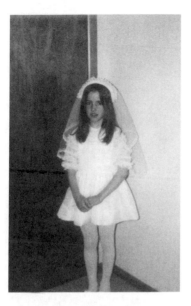

Me in my first communion
dress, Custer, South
Dakota, circa 1971.

Left to right: Iris, Thomas, and me on horseback at
Mountain Ranch, 1969. I'm riding Trigger.

Bloody Mary

My friend Deana at Lake
Elmo, Minnesota, circa 1974.

My brothers Thomas and Sam and our dog Lobo in
front of our barn at Lake Elmo, Minnesota, circa 1973.

Left to right: my brothers Sam, Dan (in back), and Randall,
and our dog Rascal, at Lake Elmo, Minnesota, circa 1973.

**Leprechauns and
Sugar Cookies**

Grandma Dorrie at
age eighteen.

217

Grandma Dorrie and Grandpa Haraldson's house in southern Minnesota.

*Mrs. Baits, the woman who lived at
Grandma and Grandpa Haraldson's house.*

Christmas Day at Grandma and Grandpa Haraldson's house in the early 1980s. Left to right: my sister Maggie, brother Thomas (at piano), and sister Betsy.

Playing London Bridge at Grandma and Grandpa Haraldson's house, circa 1967. Left to right: Unidentified girl, me, and my sisters Maggie and Betsy.

The Ghost Girl

The antique seed poster door from the dirt room.

Graduation photo, Class of 1907, Hastings High School, Minnesota. Katrina Hartnett is in the center of the front row. (Photo courtesy of the Hastings Pioneer Room. Digital restoration by Images of the Past, Stillwater, MN.)

The Haunted Trailer

My daughter Molly.
Hudson, Wisconsin, circa 1983.

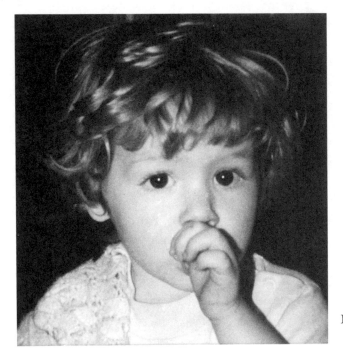

My son Jack.
Hudson, Wisconsin,
circa 1982.

Indian protection
gargoyle that kept the
ghosts away.

India "ghost in the mirror" photo. Left to right: ghost face, Jo, and
Ivy. Jo and Ivy did not see the face at the time they took the picture.

Room 5

Staircase at the Trempealeau Hotel, Trempealeau, Wisconsin, 2008.

House of Spirits and Whispers
The True Story of a Haunted House

ANNIE WILDER

Annie Wilder suspected the funky 100-year-old house was haunted when she saw it for the first time. But nothing could have prepared her for the mischievous and downright scary antics that take place once she, her two children, and her cats move into the rundown Victorian home. Disembodied conversation, pounding walls, glowing orbs, and mysterious whispers soon escalate into full-fledged ghostly visits—provoking sheer terror that, over time, transforms into curiosity. Determined to make peace with her spirit guests, she invites renowned clairvoyant Echo Bodine over and learns fascinating details about each of the entities residing there.

Wilder's gripping tale provides a compelling glimpse into the otherworldly nature of the lonely spirits, protective forces, phantom pets, and departed loved ones that occupy her remarkable home.

ANNIE WILDER (Minnesota) is a mother and writer. She continues to bravely live in her spooky old house with three cats and numerous ghosts. This is her first book.

978-0-7387-0777-8, 192 pp., 6 x 9 $13.95

To Write to the Author

If you wish to contact the author or would like more information about this book, please write to the author in care of Llewellyn Worldwide and we will forward your request. Both the author and publisher appreciate hearing from you and learning of your enjoyment of this book and how it has helped you. Llewellyn Worldwide cannot guarantee that every letter written to the author can be answered, but all will be forwarded. Please write to:

Annie Wilder
℅ Llewellyn Worldwide
2143 Wooddale Drive, Dept. 978-0-7387-1440-0
Woodbury, MN 55125-2989

Please enclose a self-addressed stamped envelope for reply,
or $1.00 to cover costs. If outside U.S.A., enclose
international postal reply coupon.

Many of Llewellyn's authors have websites with additional information and resources. For more information, please visit our website at

HTTP://WWW.LLEWELLYN.COM